Bright Unbearable Reality

Bright Unbearable Reality

Essays

ANNA BADKHEN

nyrb **New York Review Books** New York

This is a New York Review Book

published by The New York Review of Books

435 Hudson Street, New York NY 10014

www.nyrb.com

Library of Congress Cataloging-in-Publication Data
Names: Badkhen, Anna, 1976– author.
Title: Bright unbearable reality: essays / by Anna Badkhen.
Other titles: Bright unbearable reality (Compilation)
Description: New York City: New York Review Books, 2022.
Identifiers: LCCN 2022000734 | ISBN 9781681377063 (paperback) |
   ISBN 9781681377070 (ebook)
Subjects: LCSH: Badkhen, Anna, 1976– —Travel. | LCGFT: Essays.
Classification: LCC PS3602.A3597 B75 2022 | DDC 814/.6—dc23/
   eng/20220317
LC record available at https://lccn.loc.gov/2022000734

ISBN 978-1-68137-706-3
Available as an electronic book; ISBN 978-168137-707-0

Printed in the United States of America on acid-free paper.

10 9 8 7 6 5 4 3 2 1

Contents

Preface 9

Once I Took a Weeklong Walk in the Sahara 11

The Pandemic, Our Common Story 35

How to Read the Air 57

Acts of Humanity 69

Ways of Seeing 75

Bright Unbearable Reality 85

Landscape with Icarus 100

False Passives 113

Forgiving the Unforgivable 129

Dark Matter 158

Jericho 172

Notes 185

Preface

ENARGEIA, ALICE OSWALD TELLS US, is "the word used when gods come to earth not in disguise but as themselves." This is the word Oswald translates as "bright unbearable reality." Why do we find it unbearable to acknowledge what truly is? What kind of reality are we creating, that we cannot bear it?

The essays in this collection, which I composed between 2017 and 2021, aim to acknowledge what both separates and binds us at a time when one in seven people has left their birthplace, when of the estimated billion migrants living on earth, a quarter has crossed political borders. Boundaries of race and religion and class and gender carve communities, often lethally, often block by block. It seems more and more that we live in a world of moral dislocation. And a global pandemic—in its third year at the time of this publication—dictates the direst season of rupture in humankind's remembering, superimposes loss and anguish onto a world that already is a map of tornness.

The great Toni Morrison said about belonging and dispossession and the notion of home: "We are dreaming all wrong." In this book I examine some of our broken synapses. Maybe we can never make them whole entirely, but we can try to acknowledge and repair them, even if the sutures show, the scars of our efforts to dream differently.

Once I Took a Weeklong Walk in the Sahara

LATER WE WILL slow down to walking speed: a day of dunes, a day of black lava pavement, a day of maroon pebbles. But when we first arrive in the Sahara, Sid'Ahmed in the lead truck smooth-talks us past checkpoints, and we drive through the desert fast on a good road. An hour of pale dunes. An hour of sunburnt grass, low and white, an old man's stubble. An hour of dust storm. Oases encircle ten-thousand-gallon pillow tanks of water, laid out like waterbeds for the giants who must roam this vastness. Every hour or so, small perfect cubes of single-room houses, clean and pastel, peep out of sand the color of the skin on the heel of your palm, that spot where the lines of life and fate close in. A newborn neatness about them. They stand alone or in clusters, each a concrete replica of a Bedouin tent, with a pyramidical roof that aims an iron spike at the sky: A scattering of dreidels, each pinned up beseechingly to heaven, as if to keep them from flying away. Or to allow you to pull them out of the desert as you would an onion, shake them free of sand: Here and there a house is choked up to the eaves. When we finally stop near Chinguetti, Sid'Ahmed orders us to shinny up a massive barchan—the first of the many dunes he will make us scale—and, at the top, informs us that a village is buried under our feet.

What is a place? A memory of our presence, a memory of our absence. A separation sets the two apart. Sometimes the severing takes the shape of a mountain of sand that swallows a village. Sometimes it is a journey, a hejira, a hajj. What is a journey for? To remember, to forget. For the next week, Sid'Ahmed will lead nine of us on foot along the route on which for centuries pilgrims caravanned from the Atlantic coast to Mecca to remember devotion, to forget sin. We will start near Chinguetti, a center of religious scholarship during the Islamic Golden Age, and for seven days we will walk through the desert westward, downwind, like the devout returning from circumambulating the Kaaba. I do not know why my fellow walkers came to the desert. I came to make sense of our partings and to remember what binds us. It is January 2, 2020, and human movement and farewells are center stage on earth. One in seven of us is on the move, including—though I cannot see them from this barchan—the thousands crossing the Sahara toward the imaginary riches of Europe. In a week, the World Health Organization will announce the first death of a novel coronavirus in east-central China, and within two months, the nanoscopic virus will commence the direst season of rupture in humankind's remembering and split us in unimaginable ways. This, too, will become ingrained in our memories. I stand on the top of a dune that once was a homeland. All around me, the desert heaves and falls.

Once upon a time, the marabouts of Chinguetti began to collect books. Some volumes they acquired on their travels to other parts of Africa, and to Europe and Central Asia and the Middle East; others were brought to town by visiting scholars and pilgrims performing the hajj. A library was born, then another. Now in the heart of the Mauritanian Sahara there are twelve, holding thousands of volumes: the Quran and the Hadith, books on Islamic law, astrology, medicine, and theology that have been copied and illustrated by hand; they say the oldest manuscript dates back to the eleventh century.

We stop at one of the libraries, the Bibliotheque al Habott. It is a single-story compound of limestone slabs set a few steps down from the road. Mauritania is nine-tenths desert, and the Sahara is rising, lapping at walls; it has expanded by a tenth since 1920, in part because of the natural cycles of rainfall and wind, in part because of manmade climate change. A tin sign on the roof announces that this library was founded at the end of the eighteenth century and contains more than fourteen hundred volumes in twelve disciplines. The librarian, Abdullah

Habott—a descendant of the founding marabout, five generations removed—explains that the library abides by two rules: that it be maintained by one of the marabout's male descendants, lest it shift patrimony; and that the books in its collection never leave Chinguetti, lest knowledge seep from the town. In this way, the founder, Sidi Mohamed Ould Habott le Grand, set out to preserve memory in the desert. But the manuscripts are disappearing in place. Abdullah Habott turns the pages with cotton-gloved hands: Some pages have been nibbled by mice; some pages are bound in embossed leather cracked by drought; on some pages, mold patinates miniature drawings in gold leaf; some books have round perforations boring through them from cover to cover where termites have drilled into the pages, as if to take core samples. And some books are no longer books but powdery termite refuse, each a miniature bound desert, a sand mandala recording the way we become severed from our own past. The cartilage of history is precious and perishable: tens of millions of family chronicles of tens of millions of people lost in transit or in the slave trade, lost in translation or untranslatable, abridged out of fear or neglect or unsuitability, so that we are displaced not merely in place but also in time, our ancestral narratives mislaid or missing or hidden from our sight.

At the Habott Library, dizzied, I begin to fall down one of the termite holes, like Alice in Wonderland. I know that I am witnessing a marvel. I know that I am supposed to feel something profound. But I cannot. There is simply too much spacetime.

Sid'Ahmed marches us through Chinguetti's sand-swelled alleys, halts us at an overlook, leans on the limestone stump of an unmortared wall. A young black goat wearing a wide choker, to keep it from goring the shearer, toddles through former bedrooms; the choker, hammered from a tomato can, is inscribed: USA. Once upon a time, says Sid'Ahmed, centuries ago, this was someone's home. Chinguetti dates back to the eighth century—it is the same age as *Beowulf,* Charlemagne, the second siege of Constantinople—but the original structures are long gone; the ruins are from the thirteenth century or later, compounds abandoned by families who moved to bigger cities, with more opportunities and less sand. I cannot say if Sid'Ahmed entirely disapproves of urban migration: His family house in the regional capital fifty miles to the west, where we took our lunch, has electricity, a water pump, and flush toilets; but here he rues the encroaching desert, the carelessness of the locals who let their livestock roam free, global warming. I sense nostalgia. "Another problem," he says, "is the tourists. This ancient place they pick apart for souvenirs, stone by stone." To demonstrate, Sid'Ahmed plucks a rock from the leftover wall and tosses it underhand downhill. The stone thuds dully on sand.

Once back from the desert, I will read articles about Chinguetti that describe the city and her libraries as endangered. But aren't all of us in the world endangered? Our onward path is uncertain and perilous; our past, by and large, is a poem of erasure. The heroine sets out on a quest-journey—and when she turns around to look, the bread crumbs are gone.

What sets the ruins of Chinguetti apart from the many other ruins I have seen on other continents, in peace and in wartime, is not the desert. It is the books. Each is an intention to connect to a past and to reach into the future, each a memory of the people who wrote it multiplied by the memories of the travelers who brought it here, the people who have read it, the people who never will. I wonder how much of the sand that is swallowing Chinguetti streets is frass.

Months afterward, I hold in my hands a different book, of another desert sojourn. Yasmina Benabderrahmane's *La Bête* is a collection of Super 8 still frames captured so close up that I want to move the pages farther from my eyes, to look from farther away, from a barchan, say, to put some distance between us. Something in the book is disappearing—a valley of clay potters, a bird sanctuary, a grandmother's village in Morocco, a second cousin ill with leukemia—but the disappearance is too near to articulate, or too still to see: You can only sense it.

I look at one image after another and think, What is this? What is this? In a book insert, an interviewer calls it "the aesthetics of the fragment." This is how we find ourselves—in the desert, or anyplace: fragmented, confused by distance and proximity and loss, tricked or miraged or simply ignorant; something is disappearing as we watch, what is it, what, what?

Day One

The oasis at La Gueila sits in the lee of a terraced slope of barchan dunes. It began, says Sid'Ahmed, as a camel watering hole; eventually, some of the pits the camels had shat out took root in moistened sand, and now it is a date grove. This is where we stop for our midday meal, halfway through the day's walk. We spread our mats on the sand, recline, watch the noisy palm fronds transcribe in cuneiform shadow the accounts of caravans past. Our own pack camels wander off to water; perhaps their droppings, too, will sprout a date palm, to commemorate our insignificant passage.

The dates of La Gueila taste dense and dark, like buckwheat honey.

Day Two

We walk into a field of sand glass, little gray slivers. I pick up a few; they are featherlight. Sid'Ahmed explains that the sand was fused by the flame of a meteor that is said to have crashed here between sixty and seventy million years ago, around the time of the Cretaceous-Paleogene extinction, the fifth, what scholars sometimes call the K-Pg event. (Watch a simulation video of earth's landmass formation around the time of the supposed impact: Continents, not yet wholly parted, palm one another in geologic languor. Oceans churn.) The first Western scholars to investigate the supposed meteorite crater, in the early twentieth century, believed the meteorite to have weighed one million metric tons. The existence of such an impact has since been called into question. The ostensible crater was determined to be a natural hematite formation, and the only confirmed evidence of that skyfall is the nine-pound chunk of mesosiderite a French colonial consular official picked up and shipped to Paris in 1916. The scientific term for the mixture of iron and igneous rock that make a mesosiderite: *enigmatic.* I hold a filament of sand glass up to the sun; it is the opaque of Roni Horn's glass sculptures from the book she titled *The Sensation of Sadness at Having Slept Through a Shower of Meteors*. It, too, is enigmatic, mute. Mute, from the Greek *myein*, to be shut of mouth and possibly of eyes. Anne Carson writes in *Nox*, a threnody for her brother's final and irrevocable absenting: "Note that the word 'mute'... is regarded by linguists as an onomatopoeic formation referring not to silence but to a certain fundamental opacity of human being, which likes to show the truth by allowing it to be seen hiding."

Somewhere north of the wild glass field, the aviator and writer Antoine de Saint-Exupéry, plane-wrecked, wrote: "A sheet spread beneath an apple-tree can receive only apples; a sheet spread beneath the stars can receive only star-dust." It is impossible to wrap my mind around the heaviness of a skystone falling onto the desert from outer space, and how it might be preserved in something so weightless—and there is something exquisite about not being able to wrap my mind around things, it is like making space for the shape of a human ear, or for falling in love; I think we need to practice it more often, the unknowing.

Another version to explain the shards: Lightning fused the grains together. One way or another, the shards were skymade, as we are all skymade.

Day Three

In Islam, the concept of predestination is one of the six articles of faith, like the Oneness of God and the Day of Resurrection. The expression for this tenet is bibliophilic: *maktoob*, one says, it is written; the word originates from *kitab*, book. When the Prophet Mohammed first encountered the archangel Gabriel in the Arabian desert, the archangel, who spoke not for himself but for God, reciting verbatim God's message, ordered: Read! This command, which mystified the unlettered Mohammed, was the first word of the Quran, one of humankind's most significant books—all hailing from deserts—which continue to mystify us today.

What is written? Around me, the desert documents time in micro and macro stenographies: dunes and mountains, rocks strewn by ancient eruptions, empty whelk shells from the last subpluvial, the barometric script of bent grass on fine sand. Which of these grains remembers the footfall of the people who first walked here, more than 300,000 years ago; or the Neolithic nomads who drove their cattle here from the Horn of Africa; or the Arab-speaking invaders who first brought Islam here in the seventh century of our era? The harmattan of January blows steady from the east, from deeper in the Sahara, where each year up to 350,000 people braille the desert with their aspirant feet on their way to Libya, the main point of departure from Africa to Europe. This year, more than a third of the world's migrants whose deaths en route will be recorded will die in the Sahara, though the officials who chronicle such heartbreak concede that no annals document in their entirety these deaths, these forever-raptures, and that the number of people who plant their bones in the Sahara may be twice that of those who perish trying to cross the Mediterranean Sea. The sand grains that peck my skin as I walk behind Sid'Ahmed—have they traveled from far enough east to remember their passing?

Memory is fickle, a trick storyteller. Everything in life happens once and forever, until we will it differently, if only in our minds. Sometimes memory drifts off, jumbles the stories we tell ourselves and the past we think we know. This inadequacy is predetermined and unavoidable, a function of anatomy. Neurons hold on to memories unevenly, storing some and dismissing others, and the memories they do store are malleable, untrustworthy, even possibly untrue: our brains may create them on the fly, in the very moment of the encounter, when something indefinable in the unique and ephemeral soundboard of our cortex is strummed and resounds. Neuropsychologists call such memories *ghosts*; they call them *superposition catastrophes*. Memory is a trace, and a trace can linger forever or be erased in a minute. I have seen this happen in the desert. A wind gust—and the cleft hearts of camel prints, the footprints of cameleers and my own, the slight dark funnel mark of my piss in the concave lee of a barchan: all gone. And once they are no longer, who can say the place is the same, or that it even existed, or that we ever passed through? Then, ten paces away, the sand vanishes completely, gives way to the palimpsest surface of a *reg*, and I am walking on miniscule shells that remember when they were the bottom of a prehistoric lake. The desert perpetually erases and rewrites itself, erases and rewrites. Watch the metronomic oscillation of a bent stalk of grass compass the same distance over and over and over.

Once, for almost a year, I lived in the desert, in West Texas; it was the year newspapers announced that the Perseids would be twice as prolific as recent meteor showers: two hundred asteroids per hour. The morning after the showers, I found on the ground a painted bunting, a migrant bird. He was every color. He was dead. A shooting star, arrived. But if you pull back, if you consider earth's progress around the sun, you can argue that a meteorite's transient state never ends: It simply assumes, on impact, the larger body's orbit.

The last glaciation drenched the Sahara. You can still see, from a satellite that orbits the earth, the dry courses of the mighty rivers that veined it during the early Neolithic. You must step that far away to access a desert's memory. They say in fifteen thousand years the Sahara will be green again.

Day Four

The day before, Sid'Ahmed had ordered us up a mountain ridge that dragon-jaws out of the desert: the Zarga Mountains, elevation 2,493 feet. He had been driving us hard, harder than the pack camels, which he absolved, routed down lenient shortcuts. We had been slogging, heads sandward. Sid'Ahmed, tall, sinewy, in his late forties, wearing a flapping boubou and good hiking boots, seemed to never tire. But he was not without mercy. On the other side of the ridge, he promised, we would slow down. We would have lunch and make camp and stay two nights, not just one: We would not have to walk twenty kilometers the following day, would not have to walk at all. We tramped up the mountains in resignation.

What did we see from the top of the Zarga ridge? Huge crescent sandbanks. Dazzling dune chains neverending. A fallow rectangular melon patch, fenced against camels, that could have been the size of a stadium or of five: The desert distorts scale, tricks the eye. *Mirage*: a word that entered the English language in the year 1800 from the French to describe the phenomenon of what an eye perceives when light rays pushing through layers of air of different densities are distorted, excessively bent. Originally it referred to the optical illusion occurring in hot, sandy deserts of objects reflected on water. It obtained its figurative sense—*deceptiveness of appearance, a delusive seeming*—within a mere twelve years, such was the urgency to describe the human desire to see what we want instead of what is there.

We caught our breath on the ridge. We drank from our water bottles. Head feathers frilled by wind, a pied crow—a trickster of fables—picked apart something in the sand. After a few minutes, Sid'Ahmed grinned, plopped down on his ass, and demonstrated what he swore was the most efficient method of sliding down the slip face of a barchan.

Now we wake, pee, wash our hands with sand. Pause only briefly to watch the desert dawn explode: We are almost used to it by now, the way God must have been almost used to dawn on the fourth morning of Creation. Overnight, a small animal, maybe a lizard, left a punched tape of prints by the zip door of my pop-up tent; I read it as "I was here," the message all of us the world over leave behind, or at least try to; the only message that never changes. It is cold. I walk toward the breakfast fire, where Sid'Ahmed and the cameleers are praying toward the Kaaba. Some say the Kaaba's Black Stone is a meteorite.

The common map designation for a desert is dots, like the ellipsis. Like saying, something is omitted here. Like saying, there probably are other versions. The desert, like a book, has many interpretations, many lives.

Dots are also a common way to depict stars: omens, dreamscapes, narratives of our predestination; tokens, writes Juan Eduardo Cirlot in *A Dictionary of Symbols*, of both multiplicity and disintegration; promises that there is more to the story or that the story is fragile, endangered. *Disaster*: ill-starredness; the extinguishing of stars, starlessness; a catastrophe; end of story.

A year after my time in the Sahara, both of my parents fall ill with the coronavirus: first Mom, on January 1, on the anniversary of my crossing into Mauritania from Senegal; then Dad, on January 3, the anniversary of our stop at the oasis of La Gueila. I am in Philadelphia; they are in St. Petersburg, Russia, eight time zones and more than four thousand miles away. Two weeks pass before they begin to recover from a high fever and weakness and, in my mother's case, a nasty cough and headaches so severe she is unable to wear reading glasses or touch the hair on her head. This is before the vaccine, before any kind of specialized treatment, and for the first few days of their sickness, the scariest days, my chest feels weighted with sand. Friends offer links to medical studies for comfort: This or that symptom indicates a milder illness; this or that treatment has proven the most effective. The studies' conclusions often appear to contradict one another. The way world science is poking in the dark reminds me of desert dunes shifting, and of how tiny we are, and how unfathomable the world. I just wish there were a less sorrowful, less biblical way of being cut down to size.

I think about the people around the globe who have gone through, are going through, such impotent dread, who also, day after day, worry about their loved ones far away; those who remember and worry about and mourn the travelers who set off across the Sahara and perished, their deaths unrecorded by official ledgers. "A single person is missing for you, and the whole world is empty," writes Philippe Arriès, and each moment at least one person is missing for millions of us, often out of reach, flung apart as we are, undone transcontinentally. The grief makes it impossible to move: This is aporia, an absence of path, a passagelessness that engenders a state of powerless, immobilized confusion, of being at a loss, a no-way that is not the same as a presence, a separation of heart and will.

Yet there is something else: the connections that may fade but never disappear, the gossamer threads of intimacy we float behind us as we disperse, the kinship that may be undone in time but that our memories sustain as vivid, iridescent as a painted bunting's plumage. Picture the brief animation anthropologists sometimes use to demonstrate human impact on the planet—a pale, luminescent tapestry of roads, railways, pipelines, cables, air routes, and shipping lanes latticing a nighttime earth—except instead of physical infrastructure, imagine the other ways in which the Anthropocene connects us: the polythreaded, shimmering veil of yearning and missing and care and love.

I walk away from our campsite in the lee of the Zargas, fast or slow I cannot tell. I stop. I stay. What does it mean to slow down in the desert? No stillness is slow enough. The meteorite of Chinguetti rushed headlong into the would-be desert, then slowed down.

I stretch out on my back upon the Sahara. Of lying on desert sand Saint-Exupéry writes: "this density that I could feel at my shoulders continued harmonious, sustained, unaltered through eternity." I recall that for a while, Saint-Exupéry flew mail planes for Aéropostale airline between Toulouse and Dakar, over the Sahara, and then in Latin America, for Aeroposta Argentina, connecting people.

Next to me I spot a stunted purple flower. Who, which caravan, carried its seed here, how long ago? I watch the desert be its mineral self; I watch a sand shadow build behind the flower. The desert meddles with time. It pretends to be motionless, harmonious, unaltered. Lie on top of a barchan and you will think you see eternity. Lie long enough and it is you buried underneath.

But already, Sid'Ahmed is calling for lunch.

After the swallows' hunt, past haloed moonset, when all color surrenders to sound, the Milky Way swirls in a slow, galactic dhikr. Wind boomerangs between cliffs, threshes stars off their stalks. I stand outside my tent with a starlight-purpled book about a poet abandoned on a rocky island; I pick out the lines:

the wind

is the most distracted messenger I know

Day Five

Rock, dune, rock. A grove of Sodom's apples with their poison fruit. Turn around—or take a bite, like Alice—and the separation will take the shape of a pillar of salt: antiseptic, infertile, desolate, like the desert. A grove of *Salvadora persica* trees to clean our teeth. A camel's septum ring has ripped out, and for a couple of hours we follow the startling little rosettes of her blood drops. The sura that begins with the invocation "Read!" is called Al-Alaq, the Clot, for the "mere clot of [congealed] blood" out of which God created the first human. The Arabic word for human, *insân*, may have its root in *nisyân*, which means to forget; it also, linguists say, may come from *uns*: to be related, to be close to, to love and be loved.

At dusk, a narrow valley, more swallows. After supper— soup made with Maggi packets, bland pasta with chickpeas and carrots, dates—we linger in the large common tent. I ask Sid'Ahmed what place he considers his. Sid'Ahmed and I are close in age, and I feel that we have bonded a little, through sparring half in jest over world politics and through calmer conversation about religion and the mystery of philosophic scholarship, about having grown children, which we conduct in a mix of French and Arabic and hand gestures. I sense a contentment about him that I envy. I also envy his knowledge of place, that in the pathless desert Sid'Ahmed remembers the paths.

"My place?" The man laughs. "I'm a nomad, I don't have a place! My place, hah. Whenever I hear the words 'my place' I think of that time I went to this wedding and it was late and this driver guy said we could spend the night at his place, and he had this tiny little house that was so full of mosquitoes it was impossible to sleep."

Then, getting serious: "In Arar I have a small plot with five date palms."

Day Six

Some of the pages in Benabderrahmane's *La Bête* are glossy, some matte; most images are black-and-white, and the color images are so faded they might as well be black-and-white too. The pages in the book are not numbered and there are no captions: Like the desert, *La Bête* offers no conventional signposts. The reproductions are imperfect, just as any attempt to capture the desert is imperfect. In most images, there is something at the bottom left of the frame. Sometimes it looks like an exoskeleton of a scorpion, flesh winnowed out by wind; sometimes it looks like an inscription in an ancient tongue. Something stuck to the lens, maybe a hair, or a memory.

Where are we from, and where are we taking all of our

imperfections and memories? If the vanishing point is an asymptote, ever beyond reach, then what is the point of our path? In the last book the philosopher Gillian Rose wrote before dying, *Paradiso*, she says that accepting aporia means accepting "that there may not be solutions to questions, only the clarification of their statement," and that such acceptance is essential to a philosophic life. What does that mean in the desert? Perhaps it means to remember that each footstep is a fall arrested, that each signifies both a departure and an arrival, distance and approach; and it may also mean to behold in awe this twofold gift-curse and then to let that, too, drift from focus until motion becomes distilled into a pure prayer: not a supplication or a plea—God "needs no petition," as the mystic theologian Abdullah Yusuf Ali reminds us, "for He knows our needs better than we do ourselves"—but a remembrance of thanksgiving, an exultation evoked, what Rose calls "a constant awareness of existence... as if on each intake of breath one were immersing one's hands in the deep folds of some fine material saturated with glorious colour." And lo, on Sid'Ahmed's orders on the outskirts of M'Heirth, we clamber up another difficult dune—and before us, downslope, iridescent and sudden, shaped like a sparkling placenta, as glorious as paradise, shimmers a spring-fed pool.

For the first time in six days, I wash my face and hands with water, not sand.

The ninety-fourth sura, Al-Sharh, repeats:

> Verily, with every hardship comes relief.
> Verily, with every hardship comes relief.

Ali, the theologian, says the repeat is for emphasis—but note how the second line feels different from the first. This is what the desert teaches about place. You hold it in your eyes, you hold it in your hand, and you get to choose—and you get to choose differently each time. What depends on your choice? Everything.

The title of Al-Sharh is sometimes translated as the Solace. This sura is also sometimes called Al-Inshirah, the Expansion of the Breast.

Before we reach the source at M'Heirth, we walk through an outpost of seasonal date pickers. The date harvest runs from June to August, and the oasis is empty, a ghost town of rock shelters. Underfoot: sand, dry fronds, empty sardine tins, the trick of swallows' shadow dance. On the southwestern edge of the oasis we stop at a row of wells.

The wells are pale mortared cylinders, magnified versions of the termite holes that gouge the books of Chinguetti, rabbit holes for a full-size Alice. They are hand-dug and plastered by hand; the water inside is nacreous, misty. Here they call this kind of well *'ayn*: Arabic for eye but also a proto-Semitic word that means eye, fountain, or looking, seeing. You are a fool to think you have come to the desert to see. It is you, thirsty and vulnerable, whom the desert puts on its velvet showcase display. Lean over a well: The cataractic water is committing you to memory. Maybe that is so it will recognize you should you return.

Day Seven

Exeunt camels, enter all-wheel drives, and we are back on the straight paved road east to Nouakchott. Now, after walking for days through so much stillness, the sensation of being transported at an accelerated speed numbs the mind. Barchans, seif chains, *regs*, scarps, pale meadows of dry grass like fuzz on a plucked chicken, oases blink past. Suddenly on the road a large herd of camels. Some are merely day-old calves, wobbly and puppyish. The drivers slow down. The metal carapaces of our trucks jostle past the camels' animal confusion, and when we pass their sole herder I remember the terror, several years earlier in Mali, of walking with a herd of zebus upon an unexpected tarmac that guillotined fast and merciless through the sandy scrubland just south of the Sahara, and watching helplessly the dreadful road split the bullish herd in two. The herder, a seventeen-year-old boy named Hassan, the youngest son of a friend, scarecrowed madly in his blue robes to force the animals off the asphalt just in time for a silver SUV to whiz by toward Bamako. A war was raging up the road and the car had a bullet hole in the trunk door. The air quivered in its wake, the scent of hot tar billowed, stilled once more, and the rest of the cows lowered their heads as they crossed. Born and bred in seasonal migrations through thorn and sand and periodic grasslands since the beginning of time, the animals made up all of Hassan's family wealth, and his family's entire remembered history was branded into their pale rumps. The hooves' purchase on pavement was uncertain, as when crossing a marble floor in stiletto heels; meteorite shrapnel spilling on a *reg* must sound like this. And as our all-wheel drives finally pull out of the camel herd and speed up again toward the Atlantic coast, toward Nouakchott, I think, as I thought then, that there is something immoral about a well-paved road, and about the speed of departure to which many of us have subjugated our lives.

I remember Hassan's shoes on that day: narrow, plastic, turquoise two-dollar lace-ups with thick soles, scrawled over with phone numbers in ballpoint pen. On Sahara's southern shore, men often wrote phone numbers on their footwear—contacts of relatives, of middlemen, of lovers they have left behind—to be dialed when needed or when possible from a borrowed phone. Their shoes were dossiers, telephone books, annals of connection, impenetrable by thorn or time or termite. Consider farewells in global terms: A great number of us has said

33

goodbye to someone else, and as we part from the people who are meaningful and close—or were, or could be, or could have been—we carry with us our kinships' map legends, the tokens of our connections, as Hassan carried on his first-ever solo dry-season cattle drive a stoppered gourd with his mother's millet couscous, a blue tarp wrapped with lengths of lasso his elder brother had given him, the family's black milking calabash, his father's blessing, and his phone-book shoes. Like many men in the bush, Hassan did not write names next to the numbers, because like many men in the bush he was unlettered, so he had to memorize to whom each number belonged. But I have never seen a man dial a wrong number, because each number signifies a particular kinship stored just so in the immeasurable library of the heart, in the ever-expanding breast, in each specific part of the shoe—left and right toe box, vamp, quarter, heel counter—corresponding to a distinct thread of devotion a traveler will carry across any parting and any distance without confusion, just as I, without confusion and across any distance, carry on the underside of my eyelids the face of the one I love.

The Pandemic, Our Common Story

THE AFAR TRIANGLE is a speckled biochrome of thorn trees and rocky dirt the color of eggshell that funnels inland from the Red Sea. Seen from space, it has the shape of a womb. Afar is a womb: Fossils of the first of the human clade were found here, and the remains of some of our earliest *Homo sapiens* ancestors. Imagine, all of humankind, past and present and future—Shakespeare, my child, the baker on the corner, Nelson Mandela, our parents, Hitler—comes from this frassy boneyard.

In mid-March 2020, at the southwestern tip of the Triangle, a day's drive from Addis Ababa, I bounce from one hominin fossil site to another, tracking the ages of human prehistory in chronological order: 4.2 million years old, 3.2 million, 1 million. My guide, Ahmed Elema—a museum worker, fossil hunter, father of eight—is as old as my parents; he can identify fragments of hominin fossils that range across the Pliocene and the Pleistocene; he is also a *balabat*, a hereditary Afar clan leader. His colleagues at the National Museum of Ethiopia in Addis Ababa call him Elema; out of deference, I address him as Uncle Ahmed. But in my mind I call him Archangel, after Uriel, the cherub who guards the Garden of Eden, the dispenser of knowledge who, in the Hebrew tradition, gave the Kabbalah to the Jews. Ahmed Elema is an enthusiastic archangel, and he rattles off directions to landmarks whose magnitude I cannot entirely fathom, the way one cannot entirely fathom Eden: "*Australopithecus anamensis*, that way!" "Look, humerus, 4.2 million!" "Hard right, hard right, to 3.2 million years ago!" "Come on, this way to human evolution!"

Have you held a 4.2-million-year-old fossil? It is heavy, like eons.

We hike and drive past jade openwork of acacias and myrrh that does not so much cast shadows as trap light, makes the place seem diaphanous. The translucent scrubland fools me into thinking that I can see through it, the way we are sometimes fooled into thinking that we can see the future, and whenever people suddenly appear I think at first they are a mirage. The people who live here today herd camels and cows and goats, carry rifles, decorate their knife scabbards with harlequin beadwork, kiss one another's hands in greeting, and give directions by flicking their wrists slightly upward, as if they expect that the followers will eventually ascend. Maybe some do ascend. Nothing seems impossible in the locus of our origin story.

Each time we chance upon a group of people we stop so

they and Uncle Ahmed can exchange the latest. The latest is always the same. Coronavirus.

The Afar Triangle is a vertiginous scramble of space-time. A recent study shows that battles between viruses and their hosts determined one-third of hominin protein adaptations since prehumans' divergence from chimpanzees. These adaptations took place here, in Afar. This is where we learned to walk on two feet, to love, to kill, to mourn, to talk, to tell stories. This is the last place all of us, before we became multiple and scattered, knowingly shared the same story—until the pandemic. Not the Black Plague, not the transatlantic slave trade nor the two world wars, not the 9/11 terrorist attacks have affected everyone, on every continent, as instantly and intimately and acutely as the spread of coronavirus, uniting us as we fear and think and hope about the same thing.

I came to Ethiopia for book research that has to do with Eden. The intended purpose of this trip was to ponder human origins, our relationship with place and change, the notion of the sacred, and human movement, ancient and modern. The itinerary took months to set. But the day I landed in Addis Ababa, Ethiopia confirmed its first case of Covid-19. My journey became a real-time passage through a world undergoing a dramatic and unprecedented remaking.

At sundown I sit on a small rise to the east of the village of Bouri, where Ahmed Elema was born. The chalky tuff around me holds the petrified remains of the Herto man, *Homo sapiens idaltu*, 160,000 years old. A few paces away, my guide and a pair of cowherds, father and son, talk about what they can do to protect their relatives from the disease. At my feet are a torn rubber sole of a man's shoe and hundreds of Acheulean hand axes. I pick up an ax. It has the shape of a teardrop. I wonder what it knows. The Herto specimens that paleontologists found here had had their skulls severed from their bodies and scalped. Someone had polished smooth a child's cranium.

After a supper of bread and wild honey, Uncle Ahmed's relatives jigsaw on mats and jerricans in the spacious yard of his sister's compound and talk about the spread of the virus. The World Health Organization has just announced more recorded cases outside of mainland China than inside, with more than 167,000 confirmed infections worldwide; more than 6,600 people have died. The disease, like evolution, like geological time, has reached a scope beyond my comprehension. Two years later, after more than 6 million people will have died of coronavirus, these fatalities will seem slight by comparison: This is how brain adaptation works, and now we can observe it in real time, in ourselves. But I have no idea yet, no one does. I retire to a reed bed in Uncle Ahmed's sister's guest hut, and there, like everyone else in the world this spring, I sink into worry.

I worry about my Dad in Russia and about a close friend in the United States, both in their late sixties, both with weak lungs. I worry about Italy's empty streets and overcrowded morgues and people mourning alone. I worry about my child, whose university in Ohio has transitioned to virtual classes and closed the dormitories, and who now needs a place to stay. I worry about borders closing, and that this virus may become a political weapon for the many people in the United States and in Europe who want them closed. Are my worries very different from those of the Herto man, who lived on this land where I am now too agitated to sleep? Or from the *Homo sapiens* who followed twenty-five thousand years later, when a megadrought wiped out ninety percent of humankind? Genetic memory of cataclysms inscribes our living bones. Dad emails: "In the human remains that have reached us we must look for traces of human reactions—the reactions of living people to disappearing reality."

Then I realize that the Archangel's sister is still in the hut. She is sitting on a jerrican next to the headboard, her face close to mine. She says absolutely nothing, does not reach to hold my hand. She is just there, by my side.

Catastrophes often bring to the fore what defines our

humanness: longing, dread, succor, love. Once, in Afghanistan, on a gelid winter night in the middle of war, I spent a night in the living room of a border police detective, and the last thing I saw as I drifted off was my host, his Kalashnikov over one shoulder, gently spreading an extra blanket over me, an impromptu act of kindness, simple and immense. I understand that my hostess is bestowing upon me the ultimate gesture of comfort: that she will stay with me through my worry, until I fall asleep.

Then, at last, I sense the benediction of being human.

The farther I drive out of Afar, the more claustrophobic and frightening the world becomes. Italy reports 812 deaths from the virus in one day; Turkey, Brazil, and Malaysia report their first coronavirus deaths; President Trump calls the disease the "Chinese virus"; the United Nations suspends resettlement travel for refugees. The Ethiopian government confirms six coronavirus cases and closes all schools. In Russia, my sister falls ill. My two traveling companions, Kabir, a photojournalist, and his friend Abel, turn more subdued as our car climbs the mountains of Amhara. At each stop we learn of new cities curfewed, borders closing, international flights suspended. We pass towns where health workers demonstrate handwashing techniques to passersby at busy intersections. The US embassy in Addis Ababa posts a security alert: Foreigners in the country have been violently attacked because they are believed to spread coronavirus. My departure from Ethiopia becomes imperiled. We hear rumors that within a week or two there will be no more international flights out of Addis. We hear rumors that within a week or two the United States will no longer allow anyone entry. We cannot verify either rumor because the Internet on our phones is too slow. In the town where we stop for the night, the Internet is down altogether, and the bellhop at the hotel explains that it has been turned off to contain speculations about the coronavirus. What precious time I do get online I spend bargaining with myself, trying to calculate how long I can feasibly remain in Ethiopia, which parts of the research I can sacrifice, how much travel and learning I can cram into the time that remains.

I feel as if I am doing my book research just under the wire—but then again, it often seems to me the whole world is living just under the wire: The mark of the Anthropocene is that we keep careening toward catastrophe in our reckless pursuit of some ambition, some *one more thing*. W.G. Sebald, whose books are in the stack I have brought on this trip, returns often and with foreboding to this "clearly chronic process of . . . impoverishment and degradation," and its fallout I see everywhere in the Ethiopian countryside: in mountainsides eroding from deforestation and heedless new construction; in putrid rivers choked with refuse; in fields where marabou storks and cows graze side by side on diapers and shopping bags and plastic bottles; in the systemic drought and out-of-season rains, both consequences of the climatic destruction we leave in the wake of our avarice. "It is a characteristic of our species, in evolutionary terms, that we are a species in despair," Sebald says. "Because we have created an environment for us which isn't what it should be."

Northward to ancient Ethiopian kingdoms. Fog slinks up mountainsides, a ragged tinsel of clouds trims slopes. The Rift Valley bathes the car in scent: eucalyptus, angel trumpet, frankincense. I check my phone. Burkina Faso has recorded the first coronavirus death in sub-Saharan Africa; Bosnia's prime minister suggests confining migrants behind barbed wire as a pandemic-halting measure; my child has found shelter with a classmate in the American Midwest. We stop for a Lenten meal of injera and beans at a café where waiters hardly acknowledge us. They stand in a semicircle in front of an enormous television screen, watching Tedros Adhanom Ghebreyesus, the Ethiopian-born director general of the World Health Organization, declare coronavirus an "enemy against humanity." After lunch, Kabir, who is Kenyan, offers a Swahili proverb: *Kuzaliwa ni bahati, ku kufa ni lazima.* To be born is a blessing, to die is promised. For the next two hours, we drive in impotent silence.

Odd to be on a journey through 4.2 million years of our past at the time when humanity agonizes about our future. The story of paradise lost seems inessential now. What I urgently must remember and hold on to is that, over millennia, cast out of Eden, our ancestors made sense of the frightening and the unknown. That in the most daunting times, we remembered to reach for the decency and the goodness against which to steady the soul. That from the fossil fields of Afar, after the primeval rupture, we made it all the way here.

Suddenly, Abel slams on the brakes. "Guys," he says, "get out of the car. Look!"

The slope tumbles from the pavement into a kohl-black ravine—here at a slant, here in terraced swags seamed with rows of boulders to mark the boundaries of harvested teff fields, past an occasional outcrop of houses with zinc roofs that shine turquoise like upside-down sky—drops momentarily into a col, and then, at a distance, soars again, gathering into the nearest of the sawtooth rows of the Lasta massif that range from the color of coffee we have been drinking on the trip, to lavender, to pearl, until toward the horizon they lose depth and definition entirely, and become a sheet of scissored silver. On the other side of the road, a wooded scarp shoots up vertically from the shoulder like Jacob's ladder to the infinite lid of low cloud. The evening sun has dropped behind the mountain, and the light in the valley is liminal, a submarine blue. Only in the far distance, a single beam punches through the cloud and palms a faraway slope golden.

"Holy!" I say, and Kabir says, "The last touch of Eden," and Abel grins and says, "In the art gallery of God there is more to see."

An hour later, at last light, three serpentine miles away from the town of Lalibela, Abel brakes again. Just past a switchback, a roadside nativity: A man with two children and a teenage boy stand over a nanny goat. She has just foaled. She is licking the placenta off the kid.

At the end of the twelfth century, after Salah ad-Din Yusuf ibn Ayyub captured Jerusalem from the Crusaders, the Zagwe dynasty king Gebre Meskel Lalibela, who had pilgrimed to the Holy Land, had a divine vision. He ordered a constellation of churches hewed wholesale out of the Lasta massif and pronounced them New Jerusalem, a place of pilgrimage spiritually equal to the City of God. They say that for twenty-three and a half years, from dawn to dusk, thousands of people dug down into the basalt, excavating twelve temples out of volcanic rock with iron scrapers the size of a small skillet. They say that by night, while humans slept, angels took over to hasten their labor.

On my first morning in Lalibela I step out of the hotel and discover that angels have alighted on the town again. Their white muslin wings are mostly folded, though some billow in light wind. A faint rustle accompanies their descent. I squint to focus. They are not angels. They are mourners. The day before, a bus carrying pilgrims to a church outside town missed a turn on the narrow mountain road. Twelve people, mostly young men, were killed in the crash. The funerals will take place in the afternoon.

The processions are multiple and inundate all the streets. The mourners come down from the mountains and stream toward the cemetery at the bottom of the town. They walk five or six abreast, shoulder to shoulder. They fill the width of each road they take. They wear white netala shawls and gabi blankets. Some carry crosses and others parasols and others framed portraits of the deceased. They are of every age, many are teenagers, and all of them are as ancient as death. Approximately twenty thousand people live in Lalibela and most of them knew and loved someone on that bus, and for hours the only sounds in town are the quiet murmur of the cortege and the soft slap of cheap plastic sandals and tennis shoes and ballet slippers and espadrilles and bare feet on the macadam. Many join the bereaved as they pass. All the shops shutter, and when the processions finally pool at the cemetery, Lalibela becomes a ghost town.

Reader, I know what you may be thinking; I thought this too. But Lalibela's sorrow on this day is not a symbol nor harbinger of anything. Her singular loss does not stand for any other loss. It stands for itself. Let us honor it.

To get out of the mourners' way, Kabir and Abel and I walk up to a thirteenth-century monastery on Mount Abuna Yosef and sit down next to a priest who is supping on injera and chickpeas at the edge of a cliff almost fourteen thousand feet above sea level, legs swinging over the abyss. The sun's last rays skim the distant Simiens and comb through his sparse beard.

Before I traveled to Afar, I visited with Dr. Berhane Asfaw, the paleoanthropologist whose team discovered Herto man, to ask about Eden and the very first hominin dispersals across the Rift Valley cradle and beyond. I wanted to know what drove us: Curiosity, ambition, desire? We met in the garden of the National Museum of Ethiopia, where Dr. Asfaw has an office. Because of coronavirus we did not shake hands, and we spoke outside, not far from the bust of Alexander Pushkin, Russia's most canonized poet, whose portrait is stenciled Andy Warhol–style on a wall of the St. Petersburg apartment building where I grew up. Pushkin's grandfather was an African man born in what historians believe is present-day Cameroon, who was enslaved and trafficked to Europe, but Ethiopia likes to claim him as one of her own.

"It wasn't departure, it was expansion," Dr. Asfaw told me.

Though anatomically modern, these ancestors probably did not have the abstract consciousness of the modern human. They likely knew no yearning, no attachment, possibly had no recognition even of moving away. They just inched outward, following food resources. I guess paradise was a place of freedom from the kind of knowledge that carries with it homesickness, yen, torment; when we knew suffering we became mortal. I recall these lines from a Galway Kinnell poem:

> we will walk out together among
> the ten thousand things,
> each scratched in time with such knowledge, *the wages*
> *of dying is love.*

Perhaps all of our existence, post-Eden, is an effort to reckon with the price we pay for poetry.

I cannot see the mourners in the valley below, but I know they are there, just as I know the rest of the world is there, all of us living and dying and worrying and loving at the same time. I check my phone. The death toll from coronavirus has risen to 187 people in the United States, 372 people in France, 3,405 people in Italy, each person precious and singular.

I did go into the museum after speaking with Dr. Asfaw. At the human evolution exhibit in the basement, I saw the three Herto skulls—two adult males and a child, probably six or seven years old—and the fragmented braincase and upper jaw of *Austrolopithecus garhi*, partially reconstructed with chicory-blue binding that makes the 2.5-million-year-old skull look like a burnish-set gemstone. I saw an artist's rendition, in a palette that evokes a religious pamphlet, of the lush volcanic jungle that the Rift Valley likely was when our earliest ancestors lived there. In the painting, Adams and Eves of Afar walk upright among the birds of the air and the wild animals of the earth and the prehistoric creeping things, unaware yet of their real or perceived dominion. On the way out, I paused over the cast of the 47 recovered bone fragments of Lucy, née AL 288-1, who lived 3.2 million years ago. Because the head of the dig that discovered AL 288-1 was a white American man who liked The Beatles, she got her Western name. In Ethiopia she is Dinknesh, which means, in Amharic, "you are marvelous."

I could not take my eyes off her rib cage, the thoracic vertebrae like tiny sparrows petrified in flight, the delicate arched flutes of costae laid out under a plexiglass sarcophagus on a piece of compressed board painted black. The Ribs of Eve. It was not the bones that kept me but the space between them. The scratched surface of the sarcophagus reflected overhead lamps into a distorted smattering of light pricks and nebulae, and through the glass the black board glimmered like the very cosmos this rib cage contains.

In the apocrypha favored by some Islamic and Christian scholars, after Adam and Eve are deported from Eden, Adam, grief-stricken, rues his transgression and bemoans his banishment in verse: He creates the world's first poem. In addition to its multifaceted meaning to the old canon, Adam's Lament carries a kind of guidance: At the moment of his deepest anguish he turned to art.

I wonder about the vision of King Lalibela. What kind of faith, what kind of poetry existed within his mind? What kind of darkness was he staving off? It is said that before his ascent to the throne, Lalibela's brothers had tried to kill him with poison, and that it was during a coma that lasted three days and three nights that the future king was transported to heaven, where God and the angels told him to cut churches out of stone.

I pass the next two days in the churches.

"How is the corona situation in your country?" a monk named Abba Ayaliu asks me outside Biete Maryam, the House of Mary—according to the legend, the first built at King Lalibela's order. Abba Ayaliu is sitting on a sheep hide in the shade, reading a psalm book so old-looking it seems to be held together by a miracle; his vestments are so washed-out they remind me of a medieval guidance book for English anchorites called *Walter's Rule*: "With regard to his clothes he should consider nothing except how they might protect him from injury by the cold—I don't know what else he should be looking for, whose place it is to sit in sackcloth and ashes!" I tell him the pandemic is spreading everywhere, and that I am very worried. He nods. "Yes, we also worry about coronavirus, and we pray for all the world." Another monk, Abba Barana Selassie, promises me that anyone who visits the churches of Lalibela is safe from the pandemic, but after I walk away, I sanitize my hands.

I return to this exchange after I leave Ethiopia, when, having spent three days in jam-packed planes and deserted airports, I finally board the train from Newark to Philadelphia, where I will sequester myself in the third-floor walkup I rent alone. There are three other passengers in the railroad car and I take a seat on the port side, closest to the exit. Across the aisle, by the window, sits an elderly man in a kepi who must have gotten on at Penn Station; he, too, is traveling by himself. His eyes and mouth are open in the unselfconscious manner of people lost in deep thought, and he is so motionless I think at first he might be dead. Twenty minutes into the ride, still looking straight ahead, the man suddenly barks "You'll be fine!" in that irritable inflection older people often assume. Then he falls silent. Another half hour passes, and again, with even more indignation: "You'll be fine!" Whom is he addressing? Someone he was talking to before he boarded, a conversation that, as happens for us all, continues in his mind long after the encounter is over? Himself? God?

A writer raised with the daily devotion of prayer once described it to me as an "instance of alongsidedness," a communion. A shared story of conviction. Conceived as a replica Holy Land, Lalibela is shared conviction embodied, carved in stone: There is Biete Golgotha, the House of Golgotha, where women are forbidden entrance, and Yordanos Wenz, the River Jordan, which collects rainwater made holy by sluicing past the churches. There is Biete Lehem, Bethlehem, where bread for the holy sacrament was once baked. The cruciform Biete Giyorgis, the House of Saint George, the last of the rock churches built in Lalibela, is Noah's Ark: both the token and the promise of our survival on this planet.

In Biete Giyorgis I kneel in a crepuscular corner of the transept. Pilgrims take turns prostrating before the sanctuary, kissing the tattered argyle carpet, the walls. I can see the grooves where the basalt was chiseled hollow to convert igneous geology into a house of God. I can see where the stone changes color from pale matte to lustrous dark salmon from the hands and foreheads and lips of holystruck worshippers who have pressed against it over eight hundred years of agon and wonder.

Like me, they came here trying to make sense of what it means to be human. Like me, they were able to come here because our ancestors had persevered over millennia of strife. I place my palm on a wall that human touch has polished to a sheen: I am touching eight centuries of despair and bewilderment and hope.

I watch the supplicants first in trepidation, then in wonder, then in prayer; at last, I fall asleep, as, I imagine, others have in this church over the ages of its existence.

Day by day, town by town, Ethiopia transforms. Coffee-shop owners turn jerricans into improvised handwashing stations; hotel and store staff don single-use gloves; the government-run telecom company replaces the dial tone with a recorded coronavirus warning; the government petitions the faithful to stop going to church, a plea the faithful by and large ignore. An hour after we arrive at Lake Tana, Kabir receives a text message: All international flights out of Addis Ababa will discontinue in two days. He will fly to Nairobi the following night. I call the US embassy in Addis, but they are unable to verify or deny anything. I book a seat on what may be the last flight west, in two days. My friends and I will head from Bahir Dar to the capital early tomorrow. My sister texts from St. Petersburg: She has recovered. As shadows fall, we sit on a concrete bench by the lakeside and order a round of beers. Over the cloudy headwaters of the Blue Nile, hibiscus blossoms trumpet scarlet alarm.

That night I dream that the churches of Lalibela are being wrapped in white veils like giant netala shawls, or maybe mosquito nets, or funeral shrouds. The veils billow over the rock roofs first, then settle in place, accentuate each frieze and cornice. Mosquitoes and anxiety wake me. At three-thirty in the morning, the priests of Bahir Dar begin their chants in Ge'ez, the ancient language last spoken outside of liturgy around the time of King Lalibela.

On the evening before my flight, Abel and I take a long walk in Addis Ababa. If walking through sequential colonies of protohuman fossils in Afar was like watching a time-lapse of the birth of a diamond, then walking anyplace else this dread spring heralds the birth of an epoch-making language born of inadequacy and tenderness and grief.

Outside the Ras Hotel, where Nelson Mandela stayed in 1962 before returning to South Africa to endure twenty-seven years of confinement, two men in business suits and Oxford shoes teach me a footshake that is part football scissor kick, part crane mating dance. At the Hilton, where I stop to use the restroom, the security guard checks my temperature instead of my bag. Abel teaches me my first phrase in Amharic: *mahibarawi reqat*—social distancing. The woman he is dating gives me a bottle of hand sanitizer as a souvenir. Fewer than three months after it was first diagnosed, Covid-19 has infected more than four hundred thousand people worldwide; within a week, that number will triple. Outside the national stadium, where a detergent manufacturer promotes its sanitizing products to the blare of Ethiopian pop, I read the latest news: In Madrid, officials have converted an ice rink into a morgue.

Ever since I left Lalibela an image haunts me. It is a painting, on vellum, of Saint George, Ethiopia's patron saint. Several of the rock churches have at least one painting of Saint George— Biete Giyorgis, Biete Debre Sina. The painting before my eyes is from Biete Denagel, the House of the Virgins, dedicated, by some accounts, to the fourth-century maiden nuns massacred on the orders of Julian the Apostate, and by others to the thirty-six apocryphal virgins who accompanied Christ on the walk to Golgotha. This painting, I am told, is four hundred years old. Most of it is faded, and dust patinates the creases where the hide is unevenly stretched. The paint at the bottom is so badly chipped that parts of the dragon are gone entirely. But the rider's eyes are sharp, his pupils a bottomless black. His expression is not benevolent: It is all-seeing, sinister in its omniscience. He may be mourning the imminent death of the dragon, or our mortal fate.

The most dazzling object in the painting is the spearhead. The dragon slayer has drawn back the lance, preparing to strike; he resembles Orion with his sword raised in Lalibela's bright night sky. The spearhead is white-blue, like an icicle, and in the twilit church it is so bright it is almost blinding, like sea light suspended in time. Perhaps it is sea light: Saint George's earlier incarnations are as an Ugaritic mariner god who dwells in the sea, and as Uta-napishti the Distant, an immortal ancestor of Gilgamesh, who resides by the mouths of rivers. In the Quran, he is the mystic prophet al-Khidr, whom Moses summons at the juncture of two seas by placing a fish on a rock. Even as a Christian saint he retains his connection with water, as a protector of coasts and healing wells, but also—in addition to the military, skin diseases, syphilis, and several countries—as the patron saint of Castelo de São Jorge da Mina, Elmina Fortress, from which, for more than three hundred years beginning in 1482, women, men, and children were trafficked into bondage across the seas to Europe and the Americas. One way or another, the multitasking saint always tells the story of a feat; it is the moral code of the narrator that determines the ethics of the feat, and of the story.

Folklorists say oral tradition requires variation and interpretation, that we must alter the story to match the need of our times. A tale must remain fluid to stay alive, relevant. The elements must change to reflect new reactions to new realities. Millions of years after we began to become, a new virus is reshaping our common story into a faltering foundational song, a new narrative that will become stored in our bones, and which we will translate into stories of virtue or infamy over and over and carry with us across the world.

On the way from Lalibela to Lake Tana, our car overtakes an itinerant musician with a single-string masenqo over his left shoulder. He is an *azmari*—part griot, part jester, a historian-poet who documents and preserves ancestral sagas and hagiographies, who extols or berates his audience over flasks of golden honey wine. He is slogging down a mountain in cheap sandals and his clothes look more dust than cloth, as if, like with the process of petrifaction, when minerals take over organic matter until it becomes fossil, all the dust from all the roads he has traveled had taken over the fabric. And some of the dust may have been particles of straw and manure from weekly markets, or minuscule flakes of skin that the rock steps of churches and mosques have loofaed off the soles of pilgrims, or ash from coffee-shop braziers, or granules of fossilized remains of our ancestors the wind has winnowed out from the fields of Afar. The entire human history to keep him warm, and our whole future, suddenly so unscripted and fearful, his to retell and interpret from bar to bar.

How to Read the Air

I HAD PLANNED FOR WEEKS this trip to the ocean, to think
about birds. And I did go. But the night before, police officers
lynched a man in my neighborhood in Philadelphia. Then
came the insult of low and constant helicopters, and cops ter-
rorizing our streets, and curfew, and troops deployed in the
city, again. So maybe I did not think about birds the way I had
intended—though I did think about birds, impossible not to
think about birds by the ocean where they take up all the space,
where even air and water they push out of the way. Laughing
gulls, herring gulls, great black-backed gulls, Ross's gulls; terns,
oystercatchers, sanderlings, sandpipers, plovers. Ospreys.
Brown pelicans.

Why birds? Because to make sense of things this desperate
fall I have been rereading the Greeks, and the Greeks say birds
tell us what is to come.

In ancient Greece and later in Rome, augurs foretold the
future by interpreting the flight patterns and calls of birds.
Augury, in Greek *ornithomancy*, from *ornis*, fowl, and *manteia*,
divination: reading the birds for the will of the gods. Pliny the

Elder says Teiresias, the seer in the court of Thebes, invented augury. (Teiresias told Oedipus that the king was his own father's murderer.) What birds said, went. The bird savant Calchas prophesied that Agamemnon must sacrifice his daughter in order to sail his ships to win his war at Troy, and so, by most accounts, the maiden was put to death. Taking the auspices—discerning divine will from the flight of birds—makes sense because birds fly closer to the empyrean, where gods dwell, which makes the bird's-eye view closer to God's.

How to read the birds this year, this fretful year pierced by planetary sorrow and the siren call of ambulances and police cars? In the American Southwest, autumn began with migratory birds falling out of the sky, dead. It could have been the West Coast wildfires that caused the birds to deviate from millennial routes and lose nurturing layover grounds, and polluted their lungs with toxins. It could have been an unprecedented swing in air temperature, a token of climate change. It could have been a combination of factors: the Anthropocene has been killing North America's birds for some time. A year before the mass die-off in the Southwest, ornithologists reported that three billion wild birds—one bird out of four—have vanished from the continent's air in the last fifty years.

And not only on this continent. On the last day of 2019, I pilgrimed to the wetlands of Djoudj, one of the world's largest sanctuaries for migratory birds, many of them Palearctic, where a longtime game warden told me that fewer seasonal birds come each year to the Senegal River delta, and entire species no longer come at all. Cities and deserts swallow their habitats, men hunt their kin, pesticides poison their eggs. Climate change uncouples the timing of resources from the timing of migrations, syncopates their traveling cycles, puts the birds out of step with themselves. The birds are confused.

TEIRESIAS [to KREON]: I hear the birds they're *bebarbarizmenized* they're making monster sounds...

This September, after it rained dead birds, a PhD student of ornithology and phylogenetics at the University of New Mexico collected and photographed 305 bird corpses representing 6 species: 258 violet-green swallows, 35 Wilson's warblers, 6 bank swallows, 2 cliff swallows, a northern rough-winged swallow, a MacGillivray's warbler, and 2 western wood pewees. Laid out on a grid and photographed from above, the birds make a pattern like a page of text, each bird a word. The breasts and abdomens of the warblers flare startling yellow, like beacons of distress.

To know what is coming is to perceive control. And the mind is all about control, particularly in the cerebral, capitalist, goal-oriented parts of the world. We want to control, or, in neuroscientific terms, we want to exercise cognitive control, our mysterious ability to behave in accord with the goals we set. Put simply: If our cortex is informed, then (we think) we can establish a logic that can (ideally) help us predict the future so we can act in ways that (we hope) will allow us to control it—for, ultimately, we humans want to control the future, or to believe that we can. We may *say* we like to be surprised, astonished, but we like to be surprised in a particular way that is expected or suits our projected needs. This is why children like to hear the same stories: Their predictability is something to hold on to. This is why I am rereading the Greeks, whom I first read and reread as a very young child: It is like worrying a rosary or a wave-grooved seashell you keep in your pocket, something familiar for the fingers to run over and over. This is why we read projections for how long the pandemic will last, or who will win the election, or whether the global uprising against racism will prevail: We want to know when those of us who survive can go back—or actually we ought to say forward—to normal. We want to project that normal.

Three kinds of people tell us the future: prophets, scientists, and writers. One could argue that writers occupy the liminal space between the other two. The writer's impulse to draw connections, identify patterns, establish syllogisms—what cognitive psychologists call "the enormous complexity, and idiosyncrasy, of human minds, the detailed contents of which are largely unknown even to the individual concerned"—seems irrepressible, as if our neurons force us to make sense of all things, all the time. Like the bird-reading seers of ancient Greece, we cannot help ourselves.

In Islam, the word for the concept of predetermination has the same root as the word for book; perhaps this is because books allow us to foresee (they say great writers have the gift of foresight). What, then, is a prophecy? It is what is already known. Those who can interpret the writing—prophets, scholars, poets—simply make it visible to us. Joseph Brodsky (raised, too, on plentiful Greek tragedies) says literature is "a dictionary, a compendium of meanings for this or that human lot, for this or that experience. It is a dictionary of the language in which life speaks to man. Its function is to save the next man, a new arrival, from falling into an old trap, or to help him realize, should he fall into that trap anyway, that he has been hit by a tautology."

What do the birds foretell? From the shore in New Jersey I watch a murmuration of plovers skim the ocean. It stretches and compresses, tumbles, changes shape, now a horse pulling a chariot, now a goldfish flaunting a mermaid-princess tail; it narrows into a long line that glides just above the waves like a snake, then, lifting, balls up again into a sphere. Then, one after another, the birds fold their wings and plunge into the silver-banded sea. Do the plovers embody how torn we are between the noble and the base? Or maybe they are simply fishing. Three pelicans sortie on their bombing raid. The

pelicans are early harbingers of climate change; until the eighties they rarely showed up north of the Carolinas. To see them
here at the end of October, after the first frost, tells a story of
planetary-scale negligence; surely it must augur something,
too. Then a Coast Guard helicopter drones into sight, and
brings my mind back to the howling grief of Philadelphia.
Walter Wallace Jr. was twenty-seven, barely older than my children. I think of his mother, who woke up with a son one morning, and the next morning without.

A few days before I go to the ocean, I spend time with Cy
Twombly at the Philadelphia Museum of Art. Twombly
painted *Fifty Days at Iliam* in 1977 and 1978 after reading
Alexander Pope's translation of *The Iliad of Homer*; the ten
large sequential canvases were bequeathed to the museum in
1989. All but the first one are on display in one large gallery.
The first, *Shield of Achilles*, hangs on its own in a small ante-
chamber that serves as a kind of a foyer. It always unnerves me
the most. It is a vortex of crazy brushstrokes, a hurricane building, and its colors hold water and metal and blood, like a Greek
chorus, a prophecy, a premonition.

KASSANDRA: I lose my screams they find me
again!

The dread work of prophecy buckles me
down to its BAM BAM BAM...

Some of the canvases in the main gallery spell a mad violence
of names of gods and heroes of the war at Troy. But the names
of the two prophets, Cassandra and Calchas, are effaced—hers
written over and over in graphite, his spackled roughly with
palmfuls of white paint. The prophets are gone. Birds appear
and vanish, and no one is there to interpret their flight.

KLYTAIMESTRA [of KASSANDRA]: Does she talk only
    "barbarian"—those
weird bird sounds?
Does she have a brain?

When I drive back from the beach, a cardinal flies alongside
the car for a bit, opening her wings then closing them, opening
and closing, always catching herself just in time to keep going,
stringing invisible scarlet swags through the autumn bush.
That flight pattern, I once read, is called flap-bounding. I do
not know what it means. It is very beautiful to behold.

The Talmud says there was in Judea a rabbi who counted among his friends the immortal prophet Elijah. During his earthly tenure, in the ninth century before the common era, Elijah had raised the dead, received nourishment from desert ravens, brought down rain and fire from the sky, parted waters with his cloak, and finally ascended to everlasting life in heaven. But from time to time he returns to earth; maybe he is lonely for mortal company. They say he fights against social injustice. So one day, about a thousand years after Elijah's ascension, he and the rabbi took a stroll through a busy marketplace, and the rabbi asked the prophet if anyone among the people gathered there belonged in the World to Come. Elijah pointed out two brothers. The rabbi caught up with them and asked what they did for a living. We are *badkhenim*, they said, poet-jesters. We cheer up the sad.

The sages interpret the fable thusly: To truly pray we must first achieve a state of exultation, which means that joy, not sorrow, brings man closer to God. And poets help us make our prayers heard.

What does it mean to cheer up the sad, now? I would like to ask my *badkhen* ancestors, who survived dispersals and deportations and pogroms, but all the poets in my line are gone. An older colleague tells me that the role of a writer in America today is to help readers be less afraid. But I am also afraid. I am afraid for the lives of my neighbors in West Philadelphia, afraid for the lives of my loved ones around the globe, afraid for the health and soul of the world. Was Euripides afraid, or Sophocles, writing during the twenty-seven years of the Peloponnesian War? Their books do not help me feel fearless. They help me to better articulate the sorrow, not so that I can see a path ahead but so that I can have the strength to take it. They remind me, from twenty-five hundred years back—before the Black Plague, the genocide of the Americas, the Middle Passage, and the Holocaust—that for the most part, with great sorrow, and on occasion with great unexpected delight, we, those of us not destroyed en route, have caught ourselves just in time to keep going.

Homer said we ride into the future facing the past. Maybe the simplest prophecy is that we have made it this far. "But trust the hours. Haven't they / carried you everywhere, up to now?" writes Galway Kinnell. In *Economy of the Unlost*, Anne Carson's meditation on two other lyric poets, Paul Celan and Simonides of Keos, she puts it this way: "A poet is someone who traffics in survival."

The morning before returning to Philadelphia, I stand on the beach. A gale blows, a nor'easter, and it is raining, and all the birds stand facing the green-black sea, the way birds have done forever in the face of a storm.

In Mali I heard that if you catch a pied crow alive and pull down its eyelids, you will find a sentence from the Quran written in Arabic on the sclera of its eyes; reading the sentence grants you one wish. But no one I know has ever caught one. Pied crows, anyone will tell you, are very hard to catch. Note that it is the bird's eye that matters, not the seer's. Many celebrated prophet-poets were or eventually became blind: Ahijah the Shilonite, Teiresias, Phineas, Homer, Surdas. Jorge Luis Borges, Robert Hayden, Audre Lorde, W. S. Merwin. *It is written*; they did not have to physically see the future themselves to spell it out.

On the last day of October there is a rally at Malcolm X Park, halfway between Walter Wallace Jr.'s home and mine. Two or three hundred people from the neighborhood, all masked because of the raging coronavirus pandemic, gather in grief and fury and disgust. A police helicopter hovers overhead, a deranged, menacing bird basking in the cold sun of autumn. Police helicopters have hovered over the neighborhood every night since the murder, and most days too. Their sustained sonic assault overlays everything, even the metallic call of night-flying geese. It is not lost on any of us that thirty-five years earlier a police helicopter hovered above this very neighborhood and then dropped a bomb on a house full of people, five blocks from where Wallace was murdered, killing five children, six adults, and reducing to ashes sixty-one homes. This helicopter recalls that other helicopter. This protest against racism and police brutality recalls the MOVE collective's protest against racism and police brutality. Neuroscience calls this kind of memory "pattern recognition." It is like predicting, except in reverse. For example, pattern recognition was why in 2003, when the United States led an attack on Iraq, every household and business in Iraqi Kurdistan kept a caged canary: People were afraid that Saddam Hussein would retaliate with chemical weapons against the Kurds, as he had in 1988, when his bombers had dropped mustard gas and nerve gas on the town of Halabja, killing five thousand people in two days. In the spring of 2003, some Peshmerga fighters even brought birds to the trenches. A war reporter at the time, I spent those early days of the dark war with a gas mask on my belt, surrounded by trilling yellow birdsong.

If the canaries foretold the deaths of the nearly 290,000 Iraqi people that would result from that invasion, it was a prophecy none of us could read.

On the sad walk back from Malcolm X Park I see a man with a bicycle standing on a sidewalk, looking up; I follow his gaze to a host of sparrows. There must be more than a hundred of them. The birds spool out of a linden tree in a long scarf that billows and contracts, and fly across the street and settle to chitter in the branches of a golden gingko on the other side—then explode out of the gingko, shaking down a foul-smelling hail of pink berries, and pull across the street again, ever condensing and expanding, shape-shifting like the plovers on the seashore, their flapping wings even noisier than their hectic chirping, almost noisier than the police helicopter—then gather to rest in a low bush near a café, but only for a second, streaming upward again toward the taller trees up the road. I laugh, and the man with the bicycle, I can hear, also laughs behind his mask.

"What are they doing?" I ask the man, as if he were an augur. Maybe I hope he is an augur.

"I don't know," he says. "They seem to be just going back and forth."

Acts of Humanity

THE WORD "MAP" entered the English language in the sixteenth century via the French from the Medieval Latin *mappa mundi*, map of the world. *Mappa*—napkin, cloth, tablecloth, signal cloth, flag—is said to be of Semitic origin, perhaps related to the Mishnaic *menaphah*, a fluttering banner, a streaming cloth. But the oldest known maps were series of hollows, scars, notches—portholes—scooped out of bone, chinked into rock. Some of them appear to depict landmarks, some the starry sky. What each map always shows is a relationship between elements of some space; what each map always implies is the observer, you. Each represents our effort to make sense of ourselves in a particular place—and thus, each charts our reach for meaning.

On my last morning in Addis Ababa, two local acquaintances and I stop at a bistro called Keli's Gourmet Burger, not very far from my hotel. We sit outside on small wrought-iron chairs and order coffee and banana beignets. None of us can imagine as yet the profound suffering the pandemic will bring, and the mind still drifts to petty things: For instance, that this

is my last chance to sit at an outdoor café for weeks or maybe
months, since Philadelphia, where I am headed, is already in
quarantine.

A man is handing out bread loaves to mendicants outside
a church down the street, and my friends—let's call them E.
and Y.—talk about how cataclysms inspire acts of humanity
and imperil the vulnerable. They talk about Ethiopia's economy, which is so dire that three million people are internally
displaced by poverty, and tens of thousands each year risk the
maritime crossing to Yemen's warscape in search of jobs. They
talk about how much worse life will become for the country's
poorest if the government imposes a curfew or bans the cheap
kiosks and outdoor markets to curb the spread of the virus.
There will be riots, says Y.

Keli's Gourmet Burger serves Eurocentric fare, burgers and
beignets and salade Niçoise, in a neighborhood where the
United Nations has its offices and expat housing. Most of the
UN foreign staff is gone and dust has begun to settle on the
fleet of white trucks stenciled with olive branches parked in a
large lot down the street: The country has closed its borders
for entry, and there are rumors that within days there will be
no more international flights. The other customers at the café
are three young Ethiopian men and a white Anglophone family
with a little girl, the parents visibly distressed because the world
is shutting down and they must decide whether to stay or leave,
and how expensive it would be to evacuate. Actually, I don't

know why they are distressed. One of the reasons I like outdoor cafés is because I can imagine the lives of strangers.

From our table I can see the tall IOM building with a banner that reads MANAGING MIGRATION FOR THE BENEFIT OF ALL; the parking lot with the dormant UN trucks; and, between them, a long stucco wall painted with maroon-and-yellow stripes in imitation Moorish ablaq, with an unmarked teal metal gate. When we leave the café E. points at the wall and says, "This is a torture place, for political prisoners."

"During the Red Terror?" I ask. The Derg junta ruled Ethiopia in the seventies and eighties, when my friends and I were children; during those years my mother, in Leningrad, would brew Ethiopian coffee, imported into the Soviet Union from the new client state.

"No," says E. "Up until now."

"Maybe they're still doing it," says Y.

Later, reading human rights reports, I will confirm that political prisoners were definitely interrogated in this place during this century; that it was once a military office building; that, in the 1960s, it hosted the Peace Corps; and that until recently, the area around it—home now to the UN quarters and Keli's Gourmet Burger—was a slum of more than a thousand households, which the government demolished to make way for multimillion-dollar real estate development, and only a third of the displaced families were issued compensation. But when I stand before the wall it is so tall that I cannot see

71

the compound behind it, even when I rise to my tiptoes: just the powdery crowns of grawa trees and a single frangipani in pink bloom. A rusted white van with a blue Nike swoosh on the side noses out of the gate and drives off, and Y. says, "Here we have a saying: May we live our whole lives and never find out what's inside."

I want to take a picture of the wall. I leave my companions by a shoeshine man and walk down the road a bit by myself, and at the end of the block I take out my phone and immediately two young men appear out of nowhere, I swear they were not in the street just a second ago. They are wearing jeans, plain T-shirts—one white, one yellow—and disposable gloves. Blue surgical masks hang slack around their necks. For a fraction of a second I think, *They must be essential workers*. They rise before me and say, very sternly, in English, "No pictures."

It is no accident, I think, that *mappa*—a cloth, a flag, an object that flaps in the wind, that shrinks and fades and stretches on a bias—connotes a kind of unsteadiness. Maps are objects that, historically, we are taught to rely on, but they are historically unreliable. Is it any surprise that we fumble as we look for the road ahead? Take, for example, the first known map to depict both North and South America, called *Die Neüwen Inseln*. The German cartographer Sebastian Münster drew it in 1550.

This map of the Western Hemisphere shows India in China and places a nonexistent sea west of what would become North Carolina, where explorers at the time envisioned a passage to the Pacific Ocean. A mapped landscape is always tailored to reflect the cartographer's desire, the way when we say "acts of humanity" we mean "kindness," though humanity is just as likely to commit atrocities. For what is a cartographer? A dreamer of worlds.

So do we map out the world: seeing our own projections, filling in the blanks with imaginary stories or leaving them blank. Some things we don't want to imagine, so we dismiss them, the way many of us and our governments dismissed the pandemic when the virus was already killing people all over the planet by the tens of thousands. Other things we'd rather not see, so we omit them, the way the Google map of Addis Ababa omits the black site behind the fake-ablaq wall, though you can see the compound plainly on the satellite image: a dozen or so rectangular roofs flanked by trees, and a paved yard in which there stand some white cars and what appears to be a white van with a rusted roof.

The second, dated, Oxford definition for map: a person's face.

Sometimes I imagine that there is a secret laboratory where scientists are working on a map that, like Jorge Luis Borges's *The Book of Sand*, has neither a beginning nor an end: It is infinite, all-encompassing of our virtues and iniquities. It holds the man handing out bread by the church and each frangipani tree in waxen bloom and all the torture chambers in every country and each rubber raft and pirogue full of people crossing the Red Sea and the Gulf of Aden and the Mediterranean and the Atlantic and the Rio Grande. I imagine that such a laboratory must be somewhere in Eastern Europe, in a World War I barracks built for Austro-Hungarian cavalry officers, though it is not on any map except the one being created in it. No global calamity, no matter how great, ever interrupts the labor of the scientists, who are constantly catching up to our transgressions and our feats, and when a scientist dies that, too, is recorded on the map, which will never be finished. The lab is subdivided into sections, and each section focuses on one particular part of the world, though I am not sure whether the parts would be physical or metaphysical. No scientist ever leaves their assigned section, and no one has ever seen the map in progress in its entirety, but I imagine that if anyone does, they would die instantly of grief-ache. Then their death also would be entered into the map, using a particular map key that has already been designed for it.

Ways of Seeing

OLGA TOKARCZUK'S *FLIGHTS* is about movement, and it so happens that I read it in motion, mostly on planes. At first, it feels like one of those airplane encounters that confirms barely six degrees of separation between you and the passenger in the next seat: Tokarczuk's unnamed female narrator and I both grew up in Eastern Europe; she studied psychology and I was raised by a psychotherapist father; both of us travel a lot, alone; I also wrote a book about life on the hoof. There is a map of my city of birth on page thirty-seven! I become giddy: It is like looking in the mirror. I delight in the affinity—delight doubly because of the exquisite intelligence of this new traveling companion, because Tokarczuk's prose is hypnotic, spellbinding in both imagination and rendering.

Then I notice: Something in the mirror is awry.

The travel Tokarczuk portrays is the stuff of airport hotels and dinner vouchers. The protagonist, a perpetual wanderer, intersperses essayistic observation on motion with sketches of other eccentric voyagers, real and fictionalized: Frédéric Chopin's sister; a Scandinavian woman who documents abuse against animals worldwide; a Russian housewife who runs away from home. This narrator is "drawn to all things spoiled, flawed, defective, broken," largely of the *Kunstkammer* variety: She lingers in museums of curiosities; several of her characters dismember and preserve dead bodies for the purposes of science or passion or for personal bemusement.

The travel I witness often happens under duress: exodus, the tribulation of exile, flight from violence or famine. I have spent my life documenting the world's iniquities, and my own panopticon of brokenness comprises genocide and mass starvation, loved ones I have lost to war, friends' children who died of preventable diseases. For nearly each elegant vignette I read in *Flights*, my world seems to proffer an evil twin, until the looking glass of the book becomes akin to a funhouse mirror: The novel smooths away much of the real-life wretchedness I know.

Atlanta to Raleigh. My plane prepares for descent over the flooded Carolina coast where Hurricane Florence had made twenty thousand people homeless and left half a million without power. I read: "Everything is well lit; moving walkways facilitate the migration of travelers from one terminal to another so they may go, in turn, from one airport to another... while a discreet staff ensures the flawlessness of this great mechanism's workings."

Honolulu to Dallas. "The flight attendants, beautiful as angels, check to make sure we're fit to travel, and then, with a benevolent motion of the hand, permit us to plunge on into the soft, carpet-lined curves of the tunnel that will lead us aboard our plane and onto a chilly aerial road to new worlds." South of my flight path thousands of migrants from Honduras, Guatemala, and El Salvador trudge northward—on foot, in overcrowded buses, on roofs of cargo trains—in pursuit of a new world of safety and dignity.

The aggregate effect is a strange and haunting polyphony. "Each of my pilgrimages aims at some other pilgrim," the narrator of *Flights* repeats throughout the novel. But where does anyone I know to be real—the hurricane victims and the migrants, my makeshift families and temporary hosts in Afghanistan, Iraq, Mali, in the frigid, mud-caked refugee camps of the Caucasus, fellow travelers who share with me their most intimate joy and grief—fit in to Tokarczuk's world of these others?

How is it possible that Tokarczuk's intricately rendered cast of characters in movement—a young husband who goes mad after his wife and son briefly go missing during a family vacation, an émigré scientist who returns to Poland to help her ailing ex-boyfriend die in dignity—does not include the transitory people who belong to the less privileged realm of forced uprooting? In *Flights*, the traveling world exists as an antipode to the sedentary world from which Tokarczuk's narrator feels alienated because she "did not inherit whatever gene it is that makes it so that when you linger in a place you start to put down roots"—but both worlds are sanitized, elite.

Halfway through the novel, a vagrant (it appears, by choice) Russian woman delivers a spell-like soliloquy about perpetual motion as salvation from suffering: "This is why tyrants of all stripes, infernal servants, have such deep-seated hatred for the nomads—this is why they persecute the Gypsies and the Jews, and why they force all free people to settle, assigning the addresses that serve as our sentences." Here, *Flights* comes closest to mapping the sedentary world I know, one that treats rootlessness as a crime, militarizes borders, incarcerates children, tears apart families. But the novel stops short of mentioning the horrors and hardships that settled states impose on people who are made to migrate. It is as if, in this hyperinformed era, chronicles of suffering are so numbingly accessible we have become inured to them.

Turn off the news
burn the papers
skip the funerals

writes Morgan Parker.

The average cruising altitude of most commercial airlines is thirty-five thousand feet. From such a distance you can imagine shrinking the world, blurring its peopled surface. "It could well be just a lump in the throat, this globe," muses Tokarczuk's narrator. And later: "If something hurts me, I erase it from my mental map."

You can also use the elevation to take in more. From thirty-five thousand feet in the sky, you can see two hundred and thirty-five miles away. Media outlets often photograph mass migration from the air to emphasize its magnitude: Here, the caravan of Central American migrants is snaking northward; there, in the pointillist nightmare of Dadaab, Kenya, one of the largest refugee camps in the world, almost a quarter of a million people who from the sky look like dots are waiting for a home, for arrival.

Ai Weiwei's documentary about the global refugee crisis, *Human Flow*, also begins with an aerial view: A bird pushes off the surface of the Mediterranean Sea, its tail feathers and feet leave the slightest purled trace of white on the water. The bird is so tiny, and the endless sea around it is so beautiful, so ineffably, indifferently blue. A jump cut—and, instead of the bird, there is an inflatable boat crammed with migrants in orange vests; the boat, too, trails white wake.

Raleigh to Detroit. The narrator of *Flights* attends, at airports during layovers, pop-up lectures on travel psychology. I search the 403-page book in my lap for the word *refugee*, for the word *migrant*. They are not there. You see? It's all about how we choose to curate our attention. Ai Weiwei could have just kept the camera on the bird.

Between trips, the book in my bag, I return to Tulsa, Oklahoma, where I am temporarily a fellow in an artist residency. My neighborhood, the Brady Arts District, bears the name of the city's most prominent Klansman and is the site of the deadliest mass lynching of Black people in the history of the United States. The window above my writing desk faces a former concentration camp where in 1921 hundreds of survivors of the massacre were interned for days. It is now a music venue, the Brady Theater, named after the same Klansman. In colder months at night, homeless people huddle against the red brick walls that once held the pogromed prisoners. When a particularly famous artist is scheduled to perform, teenagers from all over Oklahoma arrive days early and bivouac under these same walls, cast back at the homeless a distorted reflection.

Banished from the district first by the massacre, then by midcentury redlining, and now priced out of the blocks that house art galleries and yoga studios and designer bars and single, mostly white twentysomethings, descendants of some of the men and women who survived that race war live a few blocks away, in city-scale exile.

Some nights, the setting sun gilds the gable roof of the Brady

Theater with a particular sheen. A Kaddish, or a blessing, or merely the rotation of the earth set in motion billions of years ago—that slant light strokes the charnel house and all the razor wire and the walls we build to shield us from the discomfort of certain stories, from the narratives that soon will become neighbors to our own, or will become our own, or already have, or have been always.

Kahului to Honolulu: Waterfalls pour into the Pacific past the most fragrant forests in which I have ever walked, gurgle beneath a highway that during mango season must be cleared of fallen fruit by bulldozers to make the road passable. Bulldozers in Hawai'i have other purposes as well, for example, to excavate burial grounds to make room for corporations—a Walmart in Honolulu, or the hotel where I will stay in Waikiki. For the duration of my stay, vacationers and wedding guests will revel in luxurious restaurants and ocean-view rooms, and down below, under frangipani in waxy bloom, on the sidewalk that paves over the desecrated sites, dozens of hotel workers will be striking for days to demand a living wage. Grains of sand will stick to bridal slippers, to the soles of protester's shoes, to my feet, and I will think of the opening lines of a poem by Mahealani Perez-Wendt—

O, The sands of my birth
The sands of my birth
Are digging places
Are trenching places
For excavators,
Earth movers,
And shovelers

—and there it is, just below my plane, skimming the blue majesty of the ocean: a seabird taking off.

The night before I fly from Hawai'i to Dallas, it rains over Waikiki. A downpour sluices away dozens of stories of opulence and newlywed hope; bangs on the windows of students and government workers; drenches people living in inadequate tents they have pitched in city parks; and the striking hotel workers; and, beneath, feeds the roots of scented gardens and anoints ancestral bones that remain unbulldozed, before braiding into runnels that flow into the depthless ocean and rise again, as evaporation, to fall elsewhere.

"Is it more important to bear witness to beauty, or to denounce horror?" asks a traveling photographer in a José Eduardo Agualusa novel. I wonder: Is it possible to do both?

One afternoon years ago, an old hunter and I hiked up the

thousand-year-old ruins of a Kushan castle in Northern Afghanistan. The Buddhists who had ruled the Khorasan for five centuries were long gone, and bits of sheep skulls and wisps of broken pottery dotted the tall eroding walls. Below us, the alkaline desert shone white, and in that desert there were Taliban patrols and bandits, and in the domed ceramic sky above us, American warplanes were supersonic specks, and I wondered what they could see.

I asked my companion, a man old enough to have been my grandfather, whose own grandfathers had herded sheep in this desert, what he thought of the place. He said, "This is my country. It is beautiful."

Halfway between the Kushans and our hike, in the year 1207, in this same beautiful volatile desert, the poet Rumi was born and became a refugee, a child migrant fleeing a Mongol invasion. In exile, he wrote:

I am so small I can barely be seen.
How can this great love be inside me?

Look at your eyes. They are small,
but they see enormous things.

How to take a clear-eyed view of the world's complexities, how to grasp the world in its totality of dignity and shame? Can we hold all of it, grief and beauty and the rest, the way the world already does? In our multitude of stories, so relentlessly public, how do we not lose intimacy with one another? What does it mean to look past the mirror, to choose to see something truly other than what has become comfortable? To make a deliberate effort to see the world in a grain of sand, to summon the level of curiosity required to supersede the confines of our prejudice and fear?

At one point, the narrator of *Flights* finds herself gazing at a sarira, a fleck-like relic that sometimes remains after the cremation of the corpse of a Buddhist spiritual master, and wonders if the world's beaches and deserts are "entirely made up of the posthumous essences of the bodies of enlightened beings"—and acknowledges that she would never become such a grain, she was never devout enough. In this moment, her flight of imagination is so indisputably beautiful, so earnestly true, I feel that she has glanced into that immense beyond.

Bright Unbearable Reality

THE FIRST WESTERNER known to portray human suffering from above was the Flemish Renaissance painter Joachim Patinir, born in Flanders circa 1480. Patinir is considered the inventor of what we now call *Weltlandschaft*, world landscape, which shows a panoramic cornucopia of landforms and manmade habitats from an imagined elevated perspective that intentionally dwarfs the painting's human subjects.

Patinir specialized in depicting forced migration. This makes sense: Like today's world, in which one billion people are migrants, early Renaissance Europe was delineated by human movement; some scholars estimate that one in nine people on the Continent was on the move. There were refugees fleeing religious persecution, hunger, and wars; Jews and Muslims deported from southern Europe; enslaved people trafficked from Africa and the traders who trafficked them; pilgrims; Europeans en route to the new colonies in the Americas; itinerant laborers. Patinir was a migrant himself.

What did Patinir see from his imagined altitude? Atrocity. In *Landscape with the Destruction of Sodom and Gomorrah*, blazing fortresses that look as if they had just been carpet-bombed rise ridge upon devastated ridge out of a burning plain; doomed citizens run from a castle toward a river red with the reflected inferno (or maybe with blood); behind them, a row of windmills throws up its charred sails in a tragic pis aller; heaven rains fire and what is not aflame appears covered in soot—except for the bottom right section, where two tiny, insufficient-seeming angels are leading the minuscule Lot and his daughters through a tunnel into a calm and peaceful light. In *Landscape with Charon Crossing the Styx*, a diminutive, naked soul sails halfway between the blue vistas of heaven and the charred strata of hell, where demons impale, hack, and burn the souls of sinners; it is unclear to the viewer (and perhaps to the soul) just on which shore Charon's boat will end up. Maybe the make-believe elevation—this low-flying bird's-eye view—served to allow the audience a respite: Had we been eye level with this horror, we, like Lot, might have felt the urge to flee and never look back.

Using an aerial viewpoint to illustrate catastrophe quickly became convention for sixteenth-century European artists, and migration a recurrent subject.

Of the many *Weltlandschaft* renderings of migration, perhaps the most famous is Pieter Brueghel the Elder's *Landscape with the Flight into Egypt*. Brueghel, also a migrant (born in the duchy of Brabant; died in Brussels), has crowded the painting with anecdotal detail: In the foreground, two birds sit in a tree next to a broken pagan shrine; beyond, boatmen pole across a meandering river or inlet toward a wholesome distant city. There are gardens of plenty, faraway mountains, gauzy clouds. At the bottom center of the painting, the Holy Family and their donkey, as small as an afterthought, seem to be headed in the direction of a frail footbridge that spans a dark chasm, which two heavily laden wayfarers (how far have they come?) are crossing toward another who appears to be resting—maybe their companion who has already crossed, or maybe someone giving them the right of way before traversing in the opposite direction. Everyone, everything, is seen at that odd remove. Had it not been for Mary's rich carmine cloak and the shimmer of her white veil and the Christ's white bonnet, they would have passed through the landscape unnoticed, like so many migrants.

While working on a manuscript that contemplates different ways of looking at loss and migration at a time when the very intimate trauma of individual displacement has reached a global scale, I ended up spending a lot of time studying panoramic images that show tragedy from above. Since the time of Patinir and Brueghel, the bird's-eye view almost invariably has been a way to document traumatic human events, though not always for humanitarian purposes: Historically its principal aim has been to give the military a better sense of its targets of destruction, or of the destruction's aftermath; whoever has the view has the advantage. But four hundred years after Patinir, the all-seeing viewpoint once again turned to surveying disaster and atrocity in order to elicit compassion. How better to demonstrate the scale of suffering and motivate us to political action than to zoom out? Once more, the viewfinder focused on the greatest humanitarian crisis of our time: mass migration. But the more images I looked at, the more conflicted I felt. The bird's-eye view—or the roving eye of God—left me strangely uninvolved, detached enough to scroll on.

The word *migrant* first appeared in the English language in the seventeenth century as an adjective for animals that are "changing place" and was not used to describe humans until a Congregational minister did in 1807, writing about the colonial history of New Hampshire: Its very etymology dehumanizes the non-settled. The comparison persists: In 2015, *The New York Times* wrote of the photographer Rocco Rorandelli's documentation of human movement from the air: "His photos are reminiscent of aerial images of the migrations of herds." Two years later President Trump said of some migrants, "These aren't people. They are animals." Also in the *Times*, writing about a bird's-eye image of people lined up at the Moria camp in Greece (he used the word "snaking"), Teju Cole pointed out the objectification: "They are waiting to be allowed to be human."

I search the Internet for "aerial photography mass migration" and the first page of Google results is entirely about animals. Wildebeest, zebra, buffalo. I add "human" to my search and filter the results to display images only. My screen populates, first with the beadwork of thousands of people on a bridge across the Usumacinta River that divides Guatemala and Mexico, then a stripe in the Balkans' fallow fields pixelates into a column of people trudging toward hoped-for shelter, and hundreds of tiny faces stare up from a rescue boat on the Mediterranean Sea crammed so full of human bodies that I can hardly see the deck. When I squint, the bright, zigzagging worm crawling along the no-man's-land between Greece and Macedonia in a drone image from 2015 proves to be women and men waiting in line to enter a temporary camp.

Reader, were you perhaps among the pilgrims? It is impossible, from such a distance, to see your individual yearning for deliverance from hardship, the splendor of your loving, the fracture of your farewells.

Of the estimated billion migrants living on earth today, one quarter have crossed political borders, some with the miraculous good fortune of legal endorsement by their destination states; I am one of them, I moved from Russia to the United States in 2004. If we were to be corralled into one country, its frontiers would comprise the fifth most populous nation in the world.

The first camp for migrants I visited, in April 2001, lay on a prairie outside Agjabedi, Azerbaijan. It was a temporary home to 3,358 refugees from the war in Nagorno-Karabakh, Europe's oldest ongoing armed conflict that, by then, had claimed 30,000 lives. The people had arrived at the camp in the early 1990s and scooped shallow caves out of the prairie, hanging bright crimson carpets on the walls so that clumps of dry soil would not fall on their beds. Like the Little Prince, who began each day by pulling out baobab sprouts on his tiny planet, each daybreak they swept out the snakes and frogs that had crawled into their caves overnight. The day I stopped by, the dugouts were damp. In a cave that belonged to a man named Rashid, we warmed our fingers against glass cups of hot tea.

The conflict over Nagorno-Karabakh began in 1988, when in the Soviet Union aerial war photography was still typically classified. I have never seen aerial photographs of the Agjabedi refugee camp. What would they have shown? Mud. Grass. Errant sheep ambling past bits of plastic the residents had pinned to the ground with bricks, to keep waterlogged earth from leaking onto their beds. Hard to capture from the air the waiting for years in underground caves for a war to end.

"We assume that if we can raise ourselves high enough, we will see clearly and understand perfectly the view beneath us," Caren Kaplan writes in her book *Aerial Aftermaths: Wartime from Above*, a comprehensive history of the use of aerial imagery to document warscapes. Elevation means looking down at things, rising above them, and so it exhilarates with an impression of power: This is why we build rooftop terraces and observation decks; why as teenagers in the Soviet Union my friends and I would make illicit excursions to Leningrad's interconnected rooftops, lifting ourselves for hours at a time above the dreary police state six stories below. But the photos of migrants from the Google page on my screen leave me feeling disempowered. I, the viewer, cannot participate in what I see. The refugees, holy and not—at least not to my knowledge, or not yet—plod into exile unassisted by my distant gaze. The rooftop deck becomes a widow's walk where the viewer-turned-voyeur wrings her hands in impotent despair until, like Lot, she moves on and never looks back.

"Proximity ignites empathy: You need to be speaking distance to that person," the documentary photographer Kael Alford tells me. Kael and I met in Iraq in 2003, where we were both documenting the early ravages of that invasion. She recalls Robert Capa's dictum: "If your photographs aren't good enough, you're not close enough." In *The Rings of Saturn*, W.G. Sebald writes about his visit to the panorama of the Battle of Waterloo (a nine-hour walk from where Patinir was born, a twelve-hour walk from where he died), alerting us to the "falsification of perspective" inherent to the sweeping view from above, a distortion not visual but emotional: "The desolate field extends all around.... Are we standing on a mountain of death? Is that our ultimate vantage point? Does one really have the much-vaunted historical overview from such a position?" I begin to think that an aerial photograph exposes the human condition twice: first by depicting the scope of tragedy we have at best allowed and at worst caused—and then by confronting us with the distance from which we have chosen to view it.

I think of Alice Oswald's book-length poem, *Memorial*, in which she winnows the *Iliad* down to "an oral cemetery... an attempt to remember people's names and lives." The result is a kind of escalating lament, both for the soldiers dead at Troy and for our inadequacy before their memory:

Thousands of names thousands of leaves
When you remember them remember this

Dead bodies are their lineage
Which matter no more than leaves

Oswald says her intention is to distill Homer's epic to what she calls the poem's *enargeia*, which she translates as "bright unbearable reality," "as you might lift the roof off a church in order to remember what you're worshipping." An aerial image, in a way, also lifts off the roof of a church to remind us of something fundamental about our souls—can we bear it?

By the 1940s, aerial photography to catalog, spy, and assess bomb damage was "a highly technical skill and art—but this was mostly of places and things," another wartime photographer friend, Alan Chin, tells me. Looking at the exceptions, one can argue that the distant gaze turns people into things: In a Luftwaffe photograph, the exhumed bodies of some of the 4,443 Polish officers the Soviet Union had massacred in Katyn Forest in 1940 are laid out like the pale corolla shed by a dead flower; thousands of Muslim refugees preparing to leave for Pakistan after the 1947 Partition of India spume like milk froth upon the soil to which they suddenly no longer belong.

It was not until the twenty-first century that aerial imagery of catastrophic events became the purview of photojournalism, readily available to a broad lay audience. Kaplan, in her book, attributes the shift to the increasing availability of images because of the Internet and the globalization of the media, and to the Western audience's widespread and unchallenged belief that it has the right to look. The Renaissance painters used distance to convey the unknowable magnificence of God's creation; an aerial photograph of a disaster displays the consequence of the unfathomable wickedness of man. Both are seductive. The more accessible the air becomes—you can buy a drone with a camera online for less than sixty dollars—the more accessible the unholy spectacle below.

Today, most aerial photographs are indeed made with drones. Often, they are made for reasons more urgently humanitarian than daily journalism: For instance, as I write this, drones in Bangladesh document the size of and conditions in Rohingya refugee camps; relief workers can access these photographs from their cell phones through cloud-based databases in order to better grasp the needs of the people they are trying to help. But drones, too, are used more and more as tools of modern warfare. President George W. Bush authorized 57 known drone strikes against suspected military targets in Africa, Central Asia, and the Middle East; President Barack Obama authorized more than 500; President Donald Trump authorized 2,243 drone strikes in the first three years of his presidency. "Protected by a buffer of continents and vast oceans, the United States wages war in such a way that most people at home do not have to think about geopolitics or casualty figures at all," writes Kaplan. Does aerial imagery desensitize the viewer? By 2014, the widespread US military slang term for images of humans killed in drone strikes was "bug splats."

When you look at a drone image, consider the layers of removal it both represents and embodies—the drone operator with the viewfinder can be on one continent, the drone and the people in its focus on another, the person viewing the resulting image on a third—and, at the same time, of the mind-numbing, horrifying compression: The drone taking a picture of an atrocity can also be the same drone perpetrating the atrocity. It is a perversion of a perversion, a frontline snuff selfie taken with a remote.

Almost twenty years after I visited the dugout shelters in Agjabedi, the violence over Nagorno-Karabakh began anew. Azerbaijan's president Ilham Aliyev directly credited weaponizing drones to target Armenian positions with a decisive military advantage during the forty-four days of fighting, which ended in a cease-fire on punishing terms for Armenia; many of the visuals of the conflict were also taken by drones. I read that Armenian forces shelled Agjabedi. I have seen no aerial photos of the aftermath of that attack, though I have seen other images of the war's destruction from above. I had not stayed in touch with the refugees I met in Agjabedi in 2001. If I saw them in a photograph made from above, I would not recognize them. Still, I kept looking.

The earliest surviving aerial photograph is titled *Boston, as the Eagle and the Wild Goose See It*. James Wallace Black made it on October 13, 1860, from the basket of a hot-air balloon at the height of two thousand feet. It shows city streets fanning out from left to right and at the top, a wharf fingering the harbor and several ships under sail. No people are visible in the picture.

I remember this image when I look at the aerial photographs made at the onset of the coronavirus pandemic. Many of them, too, show no people, or very few. These absences also signify mass human movement, an ongoing withdrawal from public space. A Google search for "aerial photography coronavirus" offers a list: "Aerial images show streets, beaches and landmarks empty…"; "Photos: The Quiet Emptiness of a World Under Coronavirus…"; "These aerial pictures show how coronavirus emptied cities…" The ellipses in the headlines seem to convey their own kind of vast continuum, an infinity of suffering.

On April 1, 2020, from the air above São Paulo, the Brazilian photographer Miguel Schincariol made a picture of five rows of graves for the coronavirus dead. The image is nearly symmetrical, like a yin and yang: two left rows empty, two right rows filled in, the middle row filled in on the top, empty on the bottom, and two people in blue coveralls placing a coffin into a grave in the center. Another person in blue coveralls is sitting—having a smoke? a breakdown?—on a filled-in grave. Off to the side stand people in white coveralls, maybe directing the workers, or praying. I can make out approximately seventeen graves in each row; from the way the photograph is cropped I understand that the rows continue in each direction, maybe for another row or two, maybe for miles. As if, not even a month after the World Health Organization declared the pandemic, the photographer foresaw the unabsorbable death toll.

As Alan Chin and I chat about the ethical complexities of aerial photography, he directs me to a photo essay he made in 2007 about a FEMA refugee camp just north of Baton Rouge, Louisiana, called Renaissance Village, where at least 1,500 people displaced by Hurricane Katrina were living in 580 trailers, Alan says, "with virtually no shade, far from any jobs, schools, or churches; minimal public transit." At the time, the residents complained that something in the camp was making them sick. Later that year, dangerously high levels of formaldehyde were found in the trailers; FEMA shut down the camp in 2008. Most of the black-and-white photographs in the essay are from inside the park: Boys astride bicycles pause for a sip of bottled water; two girls goof off on a gravel lot that serves as their communal backyard; a woman passes between rows of trailers carrying an umbrella for shade.

"I spent several days in there," Alan says. "But how do you show this is a whole artificial town versus any place with these issues?" He hired a single-engine airplane at a local airfield, eighty dollars for ten airborne minutes. The purpose was "more forensic than aesthetic or emotional," he says: to show the individual suffering in context.

Alan used only one aerial image in his essay; it is the first photograph in the sequence, an establishing shot. It shows, at least partially, ninety-two of the Renaissance Village trailers. They are parked back-to-back on short grass in three rows, with gravel and a handful of cars in between. That is all. The frame is tilted, the trailers aslant to the axis of the image, as if the photographer pressed the shutter by accident, or as if the trailers are there by accident, by mistake.

The next image, made at eye level, is of three rows of cluster mailbox units on pedestals, the kind that are made of aircraft aluminum, with sixteen compartments each, and that look like miniature high-rises on stilts. They are not in the aerial frame, and it must take some time to reach them from the trailers that are. Next to the mailboxes is a fire hydrant and a large plastic trash can; in the background, outside the perimeter of the camp, some trees. The mailbox units throw short, martially uniform ranks of shade. I try to imagine the woman with the umbrella crossing the sunbaked gravel, opening one of the narrow mailbox doors, and pulling out a letter.

Landscape with Icarus

IN SUMMER OUR MOTHERS would ship us off to the country to stay with relatives or in sleepaway camps so we could get fresh air and skinned knees, and we would return from our little seasonal migrations wider-eyed, wilder. Here, for example, are two black-and-white photographs, taken seconds apart: I am no older than ten, a summer wild child in hand-me-down corduroys and a too-small shirt on a wooden bench in front of our dilapidated dacha, matted hair stranding down to flat chest. Behind me, next to a bed of comfrey, the door to the pit toilet has come off its hinges. On a clothesline above my head, a double embarrassment: the plastic bags we would reuse in our Soviet scarcity, and my shapeless white cotton briefs. On the bench next to me, two large secondhand stuffed animals, a bear and a dog.

When my children were young, I too would send them away for the summer—from the city to the dacha, from Moscow to St. Petersburg, from the United States to Russia—and ahead of their return I would pace their rooms to make sure everything was just so, though never as diligently as my friend and former landlady Coura, who lives in Joal, a fishing port at the southern tip of Senegal's Petite Côte. As soon as school lets out, she dispatches her preteen son and daughter to her parents' place in Dakar. Two months later, before the kids come home, Coura scours every room of her three-story house that grows out of beach sand a block from the ocean, strips all the beds, beats out all the mattresses, washes the door curtains that keep the cool in and the flies out, washes the children's clothes that still might fit. In a photograph I took in 2015, nineteen stuffed animals pennon a clothesline that swags above a tiled stoop and a bed of dracaenas and birds-of-paradise. Pinned by their tails or ears, mostly shaggy teddy bears but also a few rabbits and something that might be a pig. Some of the animals have red dunce hats, suggesting gift bundles for overseas Christmases. Coura has laundered all of them with bleach, to kill germs.

The winter after I take that photograph, Joal celebrates City Day. At noon, tween majorettes begin to whirl to a loud and immemorial drumbeat up the main street filled with oily smoke from the fields where townswomen process fish. They wear short, pea-green dresses and white knee socks. Folks come out to watch the girls' earnest effort, their faces rigid with committed concentration, their endearing botched synchronicity. Because it is Sunday and no school—but also because they are enraptured—Joal's children follow the majorettes up the street, twirl also, stomp their own unshod or flip-flopped or sneakered feet to mimic the performance. Coura's kids go too, of course, and their cousins and neighbors. The main street runs the length of the narrow town, and as the majorettes dance northward toward the harbor, every side street and alley empties of children. The sudden quiet in the procession's wake brings to mind the dancing plagues of the Middle Ages; it brings to mind the Pied Piper of Hamelin. They say the vengeful piper led the town's children into a river in Lower Saxony, where they drowned. Or, they say, the piper was a human trafficker who led the children to be sold into bondage, or into indentured servitude, or simply elsewhere.

After the parade, the kids return exhausted and ravenous, wolf down their suppers of fried fish and sweet noodles, goof off in front of family TV sets tuned to soaps.

Around the time majorettes dance through Joal, Europe announces that it has somehow misplaced ten thousand migrant children who had arrived recently on their own, mostly from the Middle East, Central Asia, and Africa, to seek asylum. The following year, the United States loses track of fifteen hundred migrant children; three years on, more than five hundred are still missing. What happens when children go missing? Nothing happens, W. H. Auden tells us: the absenting

takes place
While someone else is eating or opening a window or just
   walking dully along;
[...]
In Brueghel's *Icarus*, for instance: how everything turns away
Quite leisurely from the disaster

Take a close look at the Brueghel: Where is the child, where
is Icarus? Nowhere. Only the faint plunging legs twitch their
last dance beneath the slim-crescent drift of feathers, and fingers grasp uselessly at a wave, and a vague splash forever rends
your heart.

Children sluice off the Petite Côte each year. Some disappear
into the premature adulthood of domestic labor or fishing or
fish processing; some board the pirogues of traffickers for the
far boundaries of Europe. Some of the children Europe misplaced may have come from here. Four years after the majorette
dance, the year the coronavirus pandemic seals most land borders in the world, two thousand children as young as ten,
alongside twenty thousand adults, arrive by pirogue from
sub-Saharan West Africa on the nearest European soil, the
Canary Islands—ten times the number of migrants as the year
prior. Their pirogues are plank-built on keels of single, scooped

redwood trunks, with barely any belowdecks and caulking made of powdered baobab leaf mixed with sawdust and tar. They say a quarter of all pirogues carrying people from Senegal to the Canaries do not make it across the water, and that voyagers often die aboard the ones that do; no one ashore knows with certainty the scope of the ocean's tithe.

Tallied in the sea's ledger now: Ousmane "Doudou" Faye, age fourteen. I read about him in the news. Doudou was born twenty miles upcoast from Joal, near the shallows where trap setters hunt for cuttlefish and murex. His father paid traffickers the boy's fare to the Canaries, but along the journey Doudou became sick and died. The news reports do not say what made the boy sick, or how the other men and boys in the pirogue prayed over his body, or who among them wept as they gave him a seaman's funeral, or if it was day or night. "Unsignificantly / off the coast / there was / a splash quite unnoticed," William Carlos Williams writes of the same painting, *Landscape with the Fall of Icarus*, which Brueghel made around the time traffickers began to march children to the West African coast and force them onto ships and across the Atlantic with monstrous regularity. The sea keeps the roster of the children who perished in that passage, too.

The reports do say that after the boy died, his pirogue ran aground off the coast of Mauritania, and everyone on board was arrested and deported to Senegal. A month after Doudou's death, a Senegalese court sentenced his father and the fathers of two other teenage boys aboard that pirogue, boys who had survived the journey, to two years in prison for endangering the lives of minors and abetting human traffickers.

Doudou's father is a fisherman. So was Coura's husband before he retired and became an environmental activist and lecturer. So are most men on the Petite Côte, seining coastal waters fish-strapped by foreign trawlers and climate change, hauling nets that are most often empty into boats designed for a different kind of sea, a sea of yore, when two hours a few miles offshore sufficed to bring home a boatful of oily sardines: boats not made to chase fish for twelve to sixteen hours daily, let alone to sail full of anxious men and boys a thousand miles across the Atlantic. The $450 Doudou's father paid for the boy's passage could have been two weeks' wage, or two months', depending on the vagaries of the sea, but even on good days many fishermen fathers say they want a different life for their sons: they know that in the long run, their ocean is spent. Doudou's father told the news agencies that he had hoped that his son, a gifted athlete, would eventually reach Italy and join a varsity football team.

Once, a middle-school teacher explained to me why he could never discipline his pupils.

"How dare I?" he said. "What if one of them is a future Einstein?"

What do we know about Icarus? Ovid tells us that he, like all children, was playful, that he

> raised his shiny face
> To let a feather, light as down, fall on it,
> Or stuck his thumb into the yellow wax,
> Fooling around, the way a boy will

—in short, Ovid's Icarus is fairy-tale childhood incarnate, an impeccable, irreverently astonished emergence. We all are born with such a gift and mostly forget it if we live long enough to age; then it takes pictures to remind us. Back to the black-and-white dacha photographs: In the vertical, I am twisting with an impish smirk to squint at something; in the horizontal, I am leaning against the back of the bench that perpetually shed brittle flakes of pea-green paint and depositing into my mouth what looks like the stunted subarctic raspberries the dacha's garden still eked out then. My head is tossed back, my eyes shut, my mouth open outrageously wide, not merely for what

I am eating but for the utter abandon of eating it, the world made new in this very instance of single-minded childhood, in this landscape with a messy little girl.

What will the girl do once she is out of the frame? Some common mischief or other: trespass on a dare into a neighbor's yard, give the stinkface to a boy who calls her a Yid, ride a bike to the far water pump without telling her grandmother first and get in trouble for it. Ovid says it was Icarus's playfulness that wrecked him:

> And the boy
> Thought *This is wonderful!* and left his father

But Ovid was in his sixties when he wrote *Metamorphosis*, and you know how things go with children, you remember it from your own parents' admonitions.

> No fancy steering by star or constellation,
> Follow my lead!

Daedalus warns Icarus as he fits him with the improbable gift of wings. But which child has ever truly obeyed a father's interdiction?

News reports do not say if Doudou's parents sent him off to the grandparents' when he was still little, or what kind of pranks he played. In a photograph I found, Doudou is a skinny kid with a footballer haircut, looking much younger than fourteen, his lips slightly apart, his gaze serious, throwing up a hopeful *V*.

Ovid sees Icarus's play as premonition.

> Young Icarus, who, blithely unaware
> He plays with his own peril, tries to catch
> Feathers that float upon the wandering breeze

—look, the feathers are already floating, uncatchable; we, like Brueghel, have a bird's-eye view of the landscape of tragedy, and Icarus, not quite a bird, does not.

But Icarus's was not a flight of fancy; it was a flight from captivity. His father, a master craftsman "who could set in stone / Confusion and conflict," built on Crete a prison of "deceptive twistings" for a king who then refused to let him go: Icarus was born in confinement, son of an artisan inmate and an enslaved woman. (Daedalus chose escape by air because his island captor, King Minos, had sealed off the sea.) And still today the adult world builds mazes and traps children, imprisons children and misplaces them. Children slip under invisible or stick-figured by news reports, no more defined than Brueghel's boy, and Daedalus, who kisses his son before the flight, "as fearful / As any bird launching the little nestlings / Out of high nest into thin air," who works so hard to secure his flight to a dreamed possibility, is charged and jailed for putting Icarus at risk. King Minos fortifies his walls.

Is it any surprise that children wing it out of labyrinths not of their own making?

We don't even know if the Pied Piper of Hamelin really existed, if the story of a fancifully dressed stranger entrancing a hundred and thirty children into marching out of a medieval town is true. It could be centuries-old apocrypha. Nonetheless, the town of Hamelin reenacts it every summer Sunday in an event called Rattenfänger-Freilichtspiel. Do you think it in poor taste to turn a mass abduction of children into a tourist attraction? Look at what we have done to real children in real life, what we keep doing.

Night is an African juju man
weaving a wish and a weariness together
to make two wings.

A photograph from the fifties, in color: A boy, three or four years old, stands on a railway platform in the Soviet Union. It is a cool, pale Baltic summer; the boy, too, is pale. He is wearing an ill-fitting knit cardigan and a red-and-white cap; beneath his striped blue shorts, bunching at the knees, sag the tops of beige cotton stockings. There are people on the periphery of the photograph, adults walking or standing, there is even a little girl holding a man's hand, but they are all far behind this boy, who stands in the middle of a semicircular clearance on the platform as if on a stage; it is as if they are giving him room, or as if they cannot approach him, and perhaps because of their distant presence the boy on the railway platform looks even more alone. The boy is holding something to his mouth with both hands, an apple or a piece of white bread, but he does not appear to be very interested in whatever it is, it is almost as if he has brought it to his face and forgotten it there. His blue-gray eyes are fixed on something outside the frame, not at the photographer but at something beyond, something abstract and immeasurable, like the future, and they are skewed with such concern, such seeming foreknowledge of desolation, as if they convey an intense mournful recognition of an inequitable world that will de-wing and trap a child inside a preconceived future, which may be an even worse act of indifference, of a leisurely turning away, than simply letting the child gossamer out of the frame, leaving only feathers in his wake.

Of course I cannot know any of this for sure. The boy in

the photograph is much too young to articulate any such sorrow, and obviously I am reading into the picture, taken twenty years before I was born. But I have seen this concern and this melancholy in these eyes many times. The boy is my father.

In his preface to Louise Meriwether's *Daddy Was a Number Runner*, a coming-of-age novel set in Depression-era Harlem, James Baldwin writes of "the helpless intensity of anguish with which one watches one's childhood disappear" and of "the wound made upon the recognition that one is regarded as a worthless human being." Stripped of that essential feature of childhood that is the magical unknowing of what happens next—deemed worthless of the possibility of flight—it is no wonder children vanish: It is easy to misplace someone whose future we have deemed wingless.

What does a picture capture? A moment in time, an artist's vision: a projection. It confines the child to a moment—fine. But can it help us refrain from confining a child to a projected future? Can our momentary seeing reveal what we owe a child—compassion, wonderment, nurture, love—without fixing her to a story grown-ups choose to tell?

Coura's daughter grows tall; her son starts elementary school. On late afternoons, Coura drinks sweet tea on the stoop below the clothesline, watches the kids flit about with their friends in gilded sunlight, watches beads of sweat and sand and fish scales pinion their shoulders.

If you look northwest from the stoop, you can see at the end of Coura's alley the main road where Joal's majorettes dance on City Day; one day, if that is what she wants, Coura's daughter will dance with them. If you look southeast, the asphodel sea. In late summer, after the rainy season, young children dredge the shallows with mosquito nets for shrimp. The hunt is a game; the kids squeal and spray one another with saltwater and laugh and rip their gym shorts and laugh more, and after they have sold their catch to their aunties and neighbors from recycled plastic mayonnaise buckets, they load up on hibiscus slushies and beignets, and they soar up the road in broad skinned-kneed ranks with the utmost abandon of those abrim with future.

False Passives

He didn't catch the name of the Saudi town where he was headed, where he had hoped to find work in a forge. Then again, he never did reach it.

First, he said, the smugglers beat him as he clung to the bulwarks of their open fishing boat. They ordered him and the other passengers to spit out the balance of the smuggling fee for their illicit voyage across the Gulf of Aden, $1,400 a head—$1,400 his whole family had raised over several meager harvests of tomatoes and sorghum and teff—or else they would be fodder for the heavy stacked waves that mawed and slobbered at the boat during the five-hour passage across the toppling seas. Then they threshed out the pitiable viaticum he had saved for the journey. At last, he and the other seasick travelers slammed ashore in Yemen and boarded the trucks that drove them across the desert to Saudi Arabia. But hardly had they crossed the border when Saudi border guards rounded them up and crammed them into an airplane that deported them back to Ethiopia. His entire journey—from his swallow's-nest village in Amhara, above the Afar Triangle, an arid boneyard where man was born; eastward to Bosaso, an ancient capital of cinnamon trade and now of human trafficking; across the Gulf of Aden, the world's busiest maritime migration route; across Yemen to Saudi Arabia; to Addis Ababa—took less than a week.

Seven months later, the ill-starred voyager was back by the side of Ethiopia's Highway 2, the north-to-south road that scaffolds the western rim of Afar. From the highway's west shoulder, wooded scarps clawed at infinite low cloud. From the east shoulder, mid-March fallow fields, cleft pink by seismic fissures, tumbled to parched scrublands deep below. He was not alone on the road. For miles along Highway 2, nearly at each roadside hamlet, unmarked bus stops scalloped clearings out of eucalyptus forest for young men to strand together like flotsam under giant billboards that proclaimed, "Let us stop our children from dangerous migration," "Illegal human trafficking will cost us the workforce of our youth," and "No man should be exposed to wild beasts or human traffickers."

Waiting for what here? A bus. A sign. Tailwind. The unmarked flag stops made of this road shoulder a kind of arcade, made of the road a temple, Our Mother of the Unmoored, and it was difficult to say whether the men who loitered there, on the western edge of the Great Rift, had already gone a ways on their journey or if they were just setting out.

When does a journey begin? When droughts parch the land, or mudslides take entire farms and crash them into ravines, or floods drown the crops? When herds dwindle, or fish leave for colder seas, or extraction poisons the wells? When war breaks out over resources, when political unraveling echoes the steady and inexorable deterioration of the home ground itself?

The regulatory vocabulary that international relief agencies use for assessments and calls to action describes climate migration as "the movement of a person or groups of persons who, predominantly for reasons of sudden or progressive change in the environment due to climate change, are obliged to leave their habitual place of residence, or choose to do so, either temporarily or permanently, within a State or across an international border." Relief agencies seem to have a term for nearly every state of human condition in extremis; they even have terms for terms. For instance, Integrated Food Security Phase Classification (IPC) is a name for the five-phase scale that describes the severity of food emergencies, ranging from Phase 1 for "minimal," to Phase 5 for "famine," which IPC defines as "the absolute inaccessibility of food to an entire population or sub-group of a population, potentially causing death in the short term." Alex de Waal, the executive director of the World Peace Foundation, an affiliate of the Fletcher School at Tufts University, has pointed out that "by using the term 'famine' to describe nothing less than an absolute state of food insecurity, the IPC classification system has had the unintended effect of implying that anything short of it is acceptable." Assigning bureaucratic value, as ever, devalues the dreadfulness of the thing.

Climate change, experts say, is the primary cause of human migration. And so it is in the highland villages and towns along Highway 2, in the rafters of the world, where people have grown things for thousands of years and still do, and still rely for the most part on their increasingly unreliable harvests; where arable land is rapidly ceding to unpredictable weather patterns, drought, deforestation for biomass fuels, erosion, or heedless development, often by outside powers; where poverty grinds so much human ambition to barren dust.

The Afar Triangle harrows the earth halfway between Beqaa Valley and Mozambique, the endpoints of the Great Rift Valley, a series of depressions that rent the planet's shell thirty million years ago. The East African Rift, which includes Afar, is one of these depressions.

Rift—a split, an act of splitting—came into the English language from the Old Norse *ripa*, to break a contract, in the early fourteenth century. Since the 1600s, it has been used in its figurative sense. In 1921, geologists incorporated it as a term for a place where the earth's crust and upper mantle are being pulled apart. They call it "extensional tectonics."

In either meaning, a rift is when or where things fall apart, come asunder. Afar is the southern rifting arm of what geologists call the Afar Triple Junction, a pulling apart of three tectonic plates near the Red Sea and the Gulf of Aden; a pulling apart that continues still, slowly dragging Africa away from Asia, slowly stretching the valley's girth. Step to the western edge of Highway 2 and peek over the brow of the Ethiopian Plateau that hugs Afar: The jagged pink trenches that gash the fields of barley and sorghum and teff are the recent stretch marks where the earth has yawned.

Fossils of the first of the human clade were found here, as well as the remains of some of our earliest *Homo sapiens* ancestors. This is where we began to form a relationship with place and change, and the notion of the sacred. This is where we adapted and adapted until here we were. Is it any wonder that ours is a history of leave-takings, of estrangement? These pale schismatic hillocks of our beginnings are our very first port of departure.

Who determines whether a journey is possible? The concept of "trapped populations" entered the mainstream vocabulary of environmental migration experts after appearing in a 2011 policy document. According to the International Organization for Migration, the term describes people "who do not migrate, yet are situated in areas under threat, [...] at risk of becoming 'trapped' or having to stay behind, where they will be more vulnerable to environmental shocks and impoverishment." The UN Environmental Migration Portal adds that "in the context of climate change, some populations might not be able to move due [to] lack of resources, disability or social reasons (e.g., gender issues), and other[s] might choose not to move due [to] cultural reasons, such as the ancestral links people have with their land." *Might not be able to* or *might choose not to*: How uncharacteristically vague for NGO-speak; how definition washes out into the indefinite, undefinable, actually and acutely human.

It is impossible to estimate how many people fit the description of trapped populations, writes the International Organization for Migration. "They are highly vulnerable populations, but data to inform action and protection are scarce"—though the World Bank by some means has calculated that by 2050 trapped populations will number 140 million people.

Note the adjectival construct "trapped." Linguists call such constructs *false passives*, or *stative* or *static passives*, or *resultative passives*. Trapped represents a result, but it conceals the cause, obscures the continuing fault that is creating both the climate catastrophe from which people might need to (and *might not be able to*, or *might choose not to*) migrate, and the conditions that prevent them from doing so, that force them to be static. It does not address the unabating gap between the mostly white power structures that generate and foster and exacerbate climate inequality and the mostly poor, mostly Black and Brown communities that bear its brunt.

One policy paper I read warned that "trapped populations" was a label that "may reduce or remove an individual's agency and independence in determining their own destiny." (Another term relief organizations use to describe people who cannot, or do not, leave environments imperiled by climate change is "climate hostages.") But it is the racist world order, which centers and upholds extractive industries and largely temperate-climate powers, that really does most of the determining. Scientists predict that almost one-fifth of our planet will be unlivable by 2070, at which time, unless they will have moved by then, 3.5 billion people—half of the world's population today—will live in the unlivable zone. And why would they not have moved? Trapped populations: the term ignores the cognitive rift between the axiom that migration is a primary form of climate adaptation, and the actuality that most destination geographies for migrants are responsible for the unfolding climate catastrophe and do all they can to keep out the people whose lives they have imperiled: They are doing the trapping.

Sometimes the journey doesn't begin at all, or it begins and is aborted, botched, cut short. In the summer of 2020, at the onset of the Covid-19 pandemic, the IOM estimated that nearly three million migrants were stranded at borders, in concentration camps, along migration routes, or with expired visas and work permits, often without financial or legal means to sustain themselves.

On a damp, cool week in March 2020, two colleagues and I drove north on Highway 2, pulling over every so often at flag stops where young men congregated with their cheap smokes and crotch funk and *fernweh*. First stop: Sulula.

"Good morning!"

Thumbs up.

"Do you speak English?"

"If I spoke English, I wouldn't be here."

"Where would you be?"

"America!"

"How would you get there? Would you go by boat?"

"No, that's not the proper way to leave."

"Don't listen to him, he's just talking. Everyone knows that it's the only way to leave."

"Do you know anyone who left this way?"

"Yes, two people."

"Are they okay?"

"We think so."

"Why do people leave here?"

"Look at us. What we eat is what we earn. Odd jobs only."

A minibus pulled up.

"Tell you the truth, we are planning to leave come Ramadan."

"Safe journey."

A wave.

On to Hayq, named after a mountain lake that is steadily drying because of deforestation and climate change; Alet; T'is Aba Lima. Men perched on precipices and passed around small oranges and puffed barley, and more and more flocked to the conversation and poured the grain into their palms like bird-seed—then spilled the spiced kernels as they traced with agitated fingers the compass roses of escape: Adams in the garden, naming things. Their frenzied needle arms dashed between the weary fields of home and the imagined tinsels of faraway happiness, diagrammed the escape they wished to prize from this beautiful everlasting land, their flight wingless, and, for that, all the more precious. Those two over there had sailed to Yemen and were deported; this one knew someone who went to Libya to cast for a Mediterranean boat; that one had two friends who must be in Saudi by now.

"Do you remember that kid from downcountry? He went to Sudan and then Libya and then Europe."

"Yes, but we haven't heard from him, we don't know where he is now, if he's made it or not."

The exodus—via Sudan and Libya or, more commonly, via Djibouti or Somalia (the Land of Nod, east of Eden) and then across the Gulf of Aden to Yemen to Saudi Arabia, what migration experts call the Eastern Route—is one of the most massive international human movements on the planet. One might call it Out of Africa III. The previous year, close to 12,000 people crossed from the Horn of Africa to Yemen each month, despite the dangerous sea passage and despite the war, subsidized by the United States, that has killed more than 130,000 people in Yemen since it began in 2014. Three weeks after our encounter on Highway 2, a militia in Yemen opened fire on a caravan of Ethiopian migrants seeking passage through the desert and killed several dozen people; the militia then drove the survivors to the border with Saudi Arabia where Saudi border guards shot more people and rounded up the rest into a concentration camp.

A parable I heard a lot growing up:

There is a flood. Ankle-deep water at first, and folks are crowding into cars, but one pious old man tells his family to go on without him, for God will rescue him. All the people with cars leave, and the water is up to his waist now, when a neighbor offers the man a seat in her dinghy. The old man waves her off: God will rescue him. Now the water is up to his armpits. A search-and-rescue team makes a water landing in an amphibious helicopter, yells at him to get in, get in, for

God's sake, but he yells back that he will be fine, thank you very much, God will save him. Then he drowns.

You can probably guess where this goes from here: On the other side, the old man meets God and demands to know why God allowed him to die, and God, incredulous, responds, "But I sent help for you three times!" It is intended to be a story about missed opportunities. But that might be a false premise. What I want to know is, why was there a flood in the first place?

The journey begins or doesn't begin long before the land no longer yields or the climate becomes unlivable. It begins or doesn't begin with systemic exploitation of environments and their communities, with colonial greed that is centuries old and unceasing, that continues to rift our world.

Between July and September 2019, as the wannabe blacksmith sailed to Yemen in a smuggler's boat and was deported back to Amhara, the government of Ethiopia performed the first IPC analysis to measure the prevalence of food insecurity in the country of 115 million people. The study found that 8 million people were in "crisis" (IPC Phase 3). A year later, war broke out in Tigray. Within months, thousands of people were killed, raped; more than 60,000 people fled from Tigray to Sudan, and 2.1 million more people were displaced from their homes but remained in the region. Ethiopian and Eritrean forces destroyed and looted households and food sources there. The Ethiopian prime minister Abiy Ahmed, winner of the Nobel Peace Prize, ordered Tigray blockaded to keep food aid from reaching the 6.5 million people trapped inside. Ahmed would later refer to these people as "rats."

Several months after the civil war began, relief agencies somehow performed another IPC study, which found 3 million people to be in Phase 3, 2 million in Phase 4 ("emergency"), and 400,000 people in Phase 5 ("famine"), mostly in Tigray and the adjacent northern parts of Amhara. In plain English: almost half a million people were starving to death and millions more were on the brink, and no one was allowed in to help them, and they were not allowed to leave.

Geologists sometimes call the East African Rift by its acronym, EAR. Or—because it really is not one singular trench that slashes the continent north to south but several consecutive lacerations—they call it the East African Rift System, or EARS.

Hello? Hello? Can you hear this?

Before setting out from Addis Ababa northward along the lip of the Western Highlands, my colleagues and I met with Dr. Berhane Asfaw, the paleoanthropologist whose team discovered some of the oldest-known direct ancestors of modern humans—*Homo sapiens idaltu*, known commonly as the Herto Man—and the Paleolithic archaeologist Dr. Yonas Beyene, who discovered the world's earliest Acheulean technology and its evolution. We talked about how human migration began sometime around two million years ago, when our early ancestors started using stone tools. A full million years went by before they domesticated fire. They probably had no concept of stars.

Skipping ahead a few hundred thousand years, Dr. Asfaw said, "You really wonder how the early humans got to Australia."

"Yes, but we don't know how many failed," replied Dr. Beyene. "What percentage succeeded."

The following day, we set off. We skirted Sululta, where several years earlier protests had erupted after Nestlé Waters had bought a majority stake in a bottled-water factory and proceeded to pump fifty thousand liters of water per hour, while local residents were left to travel on public transport to line up for water at a tap built by a Sudanese oil-and-gas company, or to collect water from a faucet provided by a Chinese tannery that had been accused of polluting water supplies. Just north of Debre Sina, we had to stop at the tail end of a day-old traffic jam. An eighteen-wheeler going to Djibouti had over-turned into a steep crevasse on the east side of the highway, and the police had sealed off both lanes; on our side, north-bound, the line of trucks and buses and cars stretched for miles, and shipwrecked travelers snacked on sugarcane and puffed barley on road shoulders that were by now a *ronde-bosse* of soda bottles and cigarette butts. Where was everybody headed? People shrugged, waved slack wrists: That way.

Some may have been going to Lalibela, a site of pilgrimage where a twelfth-century Ethiopian king hewed churches out of mountains, or to the ancient kingdom of Aksum, in north-ern Tigray, which within a year would become an epicenter of war and famine; some farther away, to Djibouti, to Sudan, to Yemen, beyond. But for now, everyone was just waiting. Young men hawked lukewarm water and soda; a matron walked uphill holding two orange chickens in one hand and an orange cat in another; truck drivers napped and smoked on the tarmac under their stalled rigs; a young mother scolded her exhausted toddler; an air-conditioned SUV with UN insignia zigzagged past the caravan, only to be sent back to the end of the line; a woman in a shimmering green jellaba ducked into a parked blue-and-white tuktuk for shade: The whole of human move-ment—impatient, weary, hopeful, resigned—on display on the stretch of road. And then afternoon church bells broke forth on a rise still beyond our sight, and the alarmed clang bounced back from all the hills, and it was a Lenten Sunday.

Town: Wichale, where in 1889 colonial Italy tricked King Menelik II into signing the duplicitous trade treaty that precipitated Italy's legendary defeat at Adwa. Clouds hemmed the perfumed slopes where they waited in the familiar uniform of itinerants, skinny jeans and damp hoodies drawn over faces fixed with resolve: To disclaim this land, to flee, they already had the tentative, slippery handgrip—the slip—their footing already lost or loosened; it was as if we'd encountered these Icaruses midflight. And they were midflight, watch: How they scanned the road for the bus that might take them away. How they hovered for hours under large billboards that diagramed the dreadful futures of migrants, faded lemming bodies crammed onto rafts and hurled facedown at foreign wrack lines, billboards made more frightening because children had stoned them for target practice, shredded them into exit-wound pennants, amplified their unblessed portent. How, now and then, these aspirants swaggered up to the eastern ledge where the shoulder plunges thousands of feet to the valley floor, and bent over—magnificent, dauntless funambulists—and aimed their expert spitballs all the way down to humankind's cradle, which so many have departed before: Take that! They talked with us shyly but with conviction about the crossing, but they did not wish to give us their names or to know ours, for we were of no use to them. They leaned instead on one another, in those boyful, sideway-draped embraces that are primed to turn any moment into bracing a wounded comrade from a fall.

A buffalo weaver flashed a tangerine rump above the road, and some of us looked up. From the bird's-eye view, all of us humans on Highway 2 must have appeared as roadside ephemera, our hopes unintelligible from above, unclassifiable. The silver mass of eucalyptus closed on the bird, and as we looked away from it, I met the gaze of the blacksmith. Maybe he anticipated my question, because he leaned toward me and swore that once he had raised enough money he would go back to Saudi and find a forge that would hire him, he was only sixteen, he had plenty of time to make something of himself, and his eyes were as lucid green as his mountain slopes, and as distant.

Forgiving the Unforgivable

Oklahoma to Texas

ON A MONDAY in early August I find myself spooning soil from Geronimo's grave at a prisoner-of-war cemetery in Oklahoma into a double ziplock bag I bought at Target. I will carry this soil, by car and bus, to Guachochi, a town in the Sierra Madre Occidental. There, three Mexican sisters who have recently traced their ancestry to the famous Apache medicine man are about to hold a Ceremonia del Perdón—Ceremony of Forgiveness. The soil is my gift to them.

Geronimo's grave is inside Fort Sill, a US Army base, so I must first stop at the visitor center to obtain a pass. The United States staked out Fort Sill in 1869, as a staging ground for punitive raids against the Native Americans who had survived deportation to Indian Territory, and even though the base dates back more than a hundred years, its visitor center bears the ubiquitous hallmarks of US military efficiency that scream temporariness: insulated white metal wall panels mounted on a concrete foundation and facing a parking lot paved with ankle breaker gravel. I have seen structures and parking lots exactly like this on US military bases in Iraq and Afghanistan, which also were staging grounds for raids into quasi-occupied lands; most of those are now gone. Inside the visitor center, a jovial military policeman hands me Form 118a, Request for Unescorted Installation Access to Fort Sill. This is to ensure somehow that I am not a terrorist. I enter my full name, date of birth, driver's license number, social security number, gender, race. Under "purpose of visit" I check "other."

Beef Creek Apache Cemetery was established in 1894, the year Geronimo and 341 other surrendered Chiricahua Apaches—adults and children—were transferred from a prisoner-of-war camp in Florida to Fort Sill under military escort. Here, in the foothills of the Wichita Mountains, Geronimo's insurgency against white colonists came to an end. It had begun in 1851, when Mexican soldiers massacred more than a hundred women and children in Geronimo's encampment, among them his mother, his first wife, and all three of his young children.

At Beef Creek, rows of identical upright headstones of white marble poke out of a manicured sloping field of green; think Arlington Cemetery minus the color guard. Among this impersonal personal misery, Geronimo's tomb stands out, a pyramid of granite boulders perhaps five feet tall, topped with a stone eagle. A small grove of white hibiscus and fragrant abelia screens it slightly from the rest of the burial ground.

Geronimo died in 1909, technically of pneumonia but ulti-mately of the humiliation that accompanied his imprisonment. To be a POW of the United States back then was different than Guantánamo: Apache prisoners could set up villages within the perimeter of the army base. They could marry and raise chil-dren and bury them. I check the stones. One couple lost three children in five years. Many grave markers have only one date.

Some Apache prisoners got to travel outside the wire. With Pawnee Bill's Wild West Show, which advertised his cameo as "The Worst Indian that Ever Lived," Geronimo hawked his legend at county fairs. And he was one of six Native men to ride horseback in Teddy Roosevelt's inaugural parade through the streets of Washington, DC, in 1901. When someone asked Roosevelt why he chose this "greatest single-handed murderer in American history" to join his parade, the president replied: "I wanted to give the people a good show."

To the left of Geronimo's is the grave of the sixth of his nine wives, Zi-Yeh, who died in 1904 at the age of thirty-five, of tuberculosis. To the right, the grave of their daughter Eva Geronimo Godeley, who was forced to attend one of the Indian boarding schools the US government had created to strip Native children of their roots; her school was almost two hun-dred miles away. She was twenty-one when she died, in 1911. Eva's daughter, Evaline, died at birth the year previous; she is buried here, too. Geronimo was gone by then: in February 1909 he was riding home drunk after selling bows and arrows at Lawton when he fell off a horse and was too hurt or too drunk to stand. He spent the night in winter cold before a friend found him ill the next morning. He died three days later.

It is noon. Thunderclouds are building in Oklahoma's sticky midsummer heat. I am alone at the cemetery; I take my time paying respects. The last grave I visit belongs to a medicine woman. Her name was Id-Is-Tah-Nah. Mexican troops kidnapped her from Geronimo's camp when she was a teenager and sold her into slavery to a maguey planter, who renamed her Francisca, like the medieval Roman saint who was forced into marriage at twelve and lost two children to the plague. Several years later she ran away and, after many days on foot, reunited with her kin. On the way a mountain lion attacked her and disfigured her face and hands, which she could never completely use again. She brewed tiswin corn beer and danced beautifully. Geronimo took her as his seventh wife.

Her headstone tells us none of this. It bears only her imposed name, misspelled "Francisco," and under it the words "Apache woman" and two dates, 1847 and 1901.

To erase, to force oblivion is the founding principal of the country indivisible from her foundational sins, whose standards flop in the prairie wind at the entrance to Fort Sill. Driving to Fort Sill from Tulsa, where I am staying this year, I pass the oil

wells of Cushing, owned by an energy company called Apache
Corporation. Apache Corporation was founded by three white
men in Minnesota and has no historic ties to any Native Americans other than appropriation and tangent: It picked the name
of a people whose history of anticolonial resistance to this day
titillates white prejudice, and it drilled its first wells on land
homesteaders had stolen from the Sac and Fox Nation during
the Oklahoma Land Run of 1889. This was the second time the
Sac and Fox had their land stolen by whites. In the eighteenth
and early nineteenth centuries, the French colonial government
and the United States had deported them from their original
home territory, in the Great Lakes region. They also stole their
real names, Sauk and Meskwaki, just as the Mexican planter
and the Fort Sill cemetery administrators stole, twice, the name
of Id-Is-Tah-Nah. Name theft is trendy, a timeless fashion. For
example, the United States stole the name of the Sauk resistance
hero Black Hawk for an attack helicopter. I have flown on Black
Hawks over other land under US occupation, in Iraq. Another
helicopter gunship the US Army used there was called Apache.

Geronimo's tomb has been desecrated at least twice. Less
than a decade after he died in 1909, members of Yale's Skull
and Bones—among them, allegedly, Prescott Bush, the father
of President George H. W. Bush and grandfather of President
George W. Bush—dug up the grave, cut off the dead man's
head, and brought the skull to the society's headquarters in
New Haven. A hundred years after his death, Geronimo's

descendants in the United States lost a federal suit to repatriate the skull under the Native American Graves Protection and Repatriation Act of 1990. Since that ruling, I notice when I kneel to scrape some topsoil from the plot, someone has beheaded the stone eagle on the tomb.

Two months before I visit Fort Sill I begin to document the swastikas I encounter in Tulsa, where I am a fellow at an artist residency. Two necklaces arranged in the shape of a swastika on a shelf of a souvenir shop. Two swastikas graffitied next to a playground by the Arkansas River, where I run some mornings. Another swastika spray-painted on the bike path just north of my ob-gyn's office in North Tulsa, the neighborhood to which the survivors of what is now remembered as the Tulsa Race Massacre of 1921 were evicted and where some of their descendants now live.

I will remember the swastikas on the day my hosts in the Sierra Madre wish their sorrow turn to ash and smoke in a ceremonial fire, because that day fascist thugs will riot in Charlottesville, Virginia, three thousand miles away. The fear that will drive the rioters is the same fear that had enabled Hitler, and that fear is why Geronimo is here, at Fort Sill. They caged him, they debauched his dignity, and once he had died they chopped off his head. They put an eagle on his grave and chopped off its head, too. The air over the Beef Creek Apache Cemetery grows heavy with cloud.

All the way from Fort Sill to the Texas-Mexico border I keep the ziplock bag with cemetery dirt in my lap. From the road I text Roberto Lujan, a retired teacher who grows pomegranate trees in Presidio, Texas, just across the Rio Grande from Mexico. Roberto is Jumano Apache; we met when I lived in the area for several months, before Tulsa. It was he who invited me to the ceremony and asked me to stop by Geronimo's grave on the way. We will travel from Presidio to Guachochi together. Roberto texts back: "The scars in our hearts will cauterize in the strong womb of the Sierra Madre." But I cannot let go of a different line, by Zbigniew Herbert:

> and do not forgive truly it is not in your power
> to forgive in the name of those betrayed at dawn

Texas to Mexico

Two days later, Roberto, his wife, Julia, our photographer friend Jessica Lutz, and I cross the border bridge from Presidio to Ojinaga. The Rio Grande runs fat and brown under the bridge. Her power is metaphysical, her shallow thalweg a frontier between two worlds that ooze chance and desire and suspicion and pity. When the Mexican immigration agent asks where we are headed, Roberto says, "To a celebration." His knee is jumping. He is giddy. Something has begun to uncoil.

Julia drops us off at a bus stop and returns to Presidio, and we take a bus from Ojinaga to Chihuahua City. The symbol of the bus company is a sprinting rabbit with bright red ears, a calque of the Greyhound bus dog. The TV screen above the windshield is playing *Unbroken* dubbed into Spanish, and a lady across the aisle is reading the Dale Carnegie classic, *Cómo Ganar Amigos e Influir Sobre las Personas*. The desert, Technicolor green after recent rains, rolls past my window. Somewhere in it, the bones of the victims of narco massacres pave over the bones of the victims of conquistadors' gold-fever missions and gringo scalp-hunting raids. For half a millennia, violence in this land has been fueled by colonial addictions.

On the bus I tell Roberto about the beheaded eagle on Geronimo's tombstone. He says, "That's why we're going to the Sierra Madre. We are going so we can move beyond it."

In the luggage compartment in the belly of the bus rocks the soil from Geronimo's grave.

Ciudad Chihuahua

Under puffy monsoon clouds the Chihuahuan Desert stretches and stretches on south, the grass startlingly tall after all the rains, and the ancient volcanoes in the distance stand blue and indifferent in the high-noon sun. The bus chugs past roadside salesmen who thrust at the traffic ice-cream bars, peeled mango slices, peanuts, horse saddles.

My geographical journey from Oklahoma to Guachochi follows, in a way, the southward passage of the Apache, who were driven from their ancestral lands in the prairie to the Rio Grande and across and through the desert and up to the clouds' rim at eight thousand feet. Theirs was a quest for safety. The quest of my Guachochi hosts is one family's gentle effort to overcome generational trauma. Jessica's quest is to witness and photograph and perhaps, like Roberto, to move beyond the hurt. Mine? I was invited so I would write about it, but also I am trying to learn about forgiveness.

We stop in Chihuahua City for the night. Monsoons in the mountains have washed out the faster road to Guachochi and we will need a full day to reach the town. Today is the International Day of the World's Indigenous Peoples, and the government of Chihuahua is sponsoring a free concert of Rarámuri folk artists in the main square, Plaza de Armas, between the cathedral and the government palace. We gorge on the spinning color of the women's full skirts. How long, I whisper to Roberto, before the government of Texas sponsors an Apache concert on the State Capitol grounds in Austin?

"Exactly," says Roberto.

By sunset the downtown is full of people, mostly families

with children and couples shopping or eating out, stopping to watch the folk concert, listen to mariachi bands, buy ice cream or elotes. The last city census, four years ago, counted almost nine hundred thousand inhabitants. Now, I am told, the population has swelled to more than a million people, mostly because of migrants: rural folk seeking work in the metroplex, victims of Trump's mass deportations, and increasingly desperate Central Americans willing to risk the crossing, like the young man I see on a median holding up a piece of cardboard inscribed with the words: "*Soy de Nicaragua. Ayúdame por el amor de dios.*" The *N* in Nicaragua is written backward.

When evening falls ultramarine and gentle, I notice another presence downtown: soldiers in camouflage on flatbed trucks with mounted machine guns. Now they are parked by the government palace. Now they are driving at a crawl past my hotel. Now they are lost among the many taillights of a weeknight. Cartel turf wars are ravaging Mexico, especially her Native communities. The soldiers: another reminder of the accretion of pain.

Sierra Madre Occidental

Bernarda Holguín Gámez is medium tall, in her early sixties. She is a retired civil servant at Mexico's now-defunct Secretariat of Agrarian Reform, a sometime tour operator, and the senior of the Holguín sisters. A photo of her as a seventeen-year-old shows a lean girl, her shoulder-length dark hair down, a string of beads around her neck. She still wears bead necklaces; her hair, now much longer, down or in a braid that is mostly gray. She hugs eagerly; all the Holguíns do. She wraps me in a bear hug the first time we meet. Her voice is assertive and calm, and even when she speaks in public it conveys great tenderness. As if she is grateful to you, all of you, for being here, by her side. She ends most conversations with a "God bless you" and "God bless your family."

Several years earlier, a family friend in the United States pointed out the resemblance between Bernarda's second son, Jesús, and Geronimo. Bernarda and her youngest sister, Gina, started looking at pictures. It was true: Jesús did look like Geronimo. So did their father. So did their paternal uncle. A lot.

The likeness made them doubt the family story that the Holguíns were white descendants of a French grandmother. They began to question their parents' honesty. Unsettled, Bernarda sought therapy; the counselor suggested she was suffering from epigenetic stress. Her cholesterol skyrocketed. She went on medication. Then, for two years, she went blind.

This may be the stuff of allegories, of parables.

This may be an appropriate response to the deception that underlies North America's modern creation myth.

What the sisters found, after Bernarda's vision returned and they turned their attention to family lineage in earnest, was no French connection. Instead, poring over birth records, marriage licenses, and death certificates across five Mexican states, they uncovered a genealogy that packs the continent's post-Columbian history into one family's tale of a hundred-plus years of racial cruelty, denial, and shame.

April 1882. Mexican troops wait until most men leave Geronimo's camp at Alisos Creek, then storm the camp. They bayonet and shoot at point-blank seventy-eight people, mostly women and children. They take captive thirty-three others and drive them to the stockade in Chihuahua City. Among these are Geronimo's second wife, Chee-Hash-Kish; their son, Casimiro; their married daughter, Tah-Nah-Nah "Victoriana" Díaz García; and Victoriana's firstborn, a boy. Victoriana is pregnant with her second child, a girl, who will be born in prison.

Victoriana's husband, a gringo named Zebina Nathaniel Streeter, eventually negotiates the release of his wife, their two children, and, possibly, Chee-Hash-Kish and Casimiro. The family escapes to the Sierra Madre, where they live in hiding. By June 1889, both the US and Mexican governments have put a bounty on Streeter's head for helping Apache insurgents. Then someone leaves a note on the desk of an Arizona newspaper. Streeter, the note says, was murdered by a lover, in a crime of passion.

Apache tradition says that speaking of the dead disturbs their eternal rest—and so the family would never mention

Streeter. Soon, another man's name begins to appear in public records in his place: Juan Ramón Holguín, a rural rancher, the husband of Victoriana Díaz García. An Apache medicine man from Arizona would tell Bernarda and her sisters that their last name, Holguín, means Someone Who Carries a Secret.

In 1901 Victoriana and Juan Ramón—né Streeter, says Bernarda—have a son they name Primitivo Holguín Díaz. He is Bernarda's father.

January 1883, less than a year after the massacre at Alisos Creek. Mexican troops raid Geronimo's camp in Sonora, murder seventeen people, and kidnap thirty-seven. Among the prisoners are Geronimo's fifth wife, Shtsh-She, and their daughter, Mariana Hernández, who is eight years old. The soldiers drive them to Chihuahua City, maybe to the same stockade as Chee-Hash-Kish and Victoriana. Geronimo tries to bargain for the prisoners' release, but negotiations falter. By now, Mexican soldiers have killed two of his wives and four of his children, and a quarter of the entire US Army is hunting him in the longest counterinsurgency campaign in US history. Three years later, he gives up.

"For years I fought the white man thinking that with my few braves I could kill them all and that we would again have the land that our Great Father gave us and which he covered with game," Geronimo would tell a reporter. "After I fought and lost and after I traveled over the country in which the white man lives and saw his cities and the work that he has done, my heart was ready to burst. I knew that the race of the Indian was run."

Shtsh-She and Mariana are sold into slavery to Batopilas, a colonial outpost in the Sierra Madre, about eighty miles from Guachochi. On paper, the Spanish crown abolished Indian slavery in 1542; in reality, servitude—sometimes called debt peonage—proliferated at least as late as 1908, when a gringo journalist posing as a millionaire investor was offered a Native laborer for four hundred pesos.

Eventually, Shtsh-She and Mariana escape into the dim canyons and join other Apaches ghosting in tributary gorges and mountain caves. Mariana marries a white Mexican colonel and renounces her Indian roots. In 1898, they have a daughter, Bernarda Hernández Ortiz. She is the Holguín sisters' maternal grandmother. Bernarda bears her name.

In 1943, after the death of his first wife, Primitivo marries Soledad Gámez Hernández, the daughter of Bernarda Hernández Ortiz. Do they know that they are uncle and niece, several times removed? Is this why the Holguín family is plagued by an extraordinarily high incidence of ill health—lupus, structural birth defects, cancer, depression? Or are the illnesses conversion disorders caused by generational trauma, as Bernarda believes? The mountains hold so much concave silence. Primitivo and Soledad have eight children; Bernarda Holguín Gámez is the eldest daughter. Growing up among darker-skinned Rarámuri, the siblings are taught that they are white, descendants of a French woman.

This weekend, the Holguíns are for the first time celebrating their lineage and honoring their roots in the very mountains where their ancestors had denounced and hid theirs.

We arrive in Guachochi the night before the opening event. The mountains are drenched with recent rains; between out-crops of piñon, bald rock paths shine like a lattice of quicksilver. Our rental sedan barely negotiates the rain-slicked mountain curves on bald tires and two cylinders. At one point, after ford-ing a river, it gets stuck for two hours on an unpaved upslope.

By the time we reach the Holguín ranch it is almost dark. The sisters' father, Primitivo Holguín Díaz, built the ranch in 1924; the sisters were born here. One of them, Hilda, tells me their umbilical cords are buried somewhere in the garden. No one lives on the ranch year-round anymore. There is occasional electricity and occasional running water. Tonight, lightning has knocked out power on the property and the pump is not working. In the kitchen, in the light of three gas lamps, two Rarámuri women are preparing refreshments for a crowd—a vat of canela, batteries of sandwiches, shrink-wrapped mounds of sweet buns—and Hilda, who now lives mostly in Vancouver with her children, is telling me about growing up here: the two-hour hikes to school, the mushroom hunts. We also hunted mushrooms when I was a kid, in the Soviet Union, I tell her—and then it hits me that the kitchen of her parents' home is furnished exactly the same way as the kitchen at the house my family owned outside Leningrad until the late 1980s, a summer house my maternal great-great-grandfather built around the time Geronimo surrendered to the US Army. The same linoleum tablecloths on every table and counter. The same pastel-colored plywood cabinets with wooden handles. In the walls, the same haphazard orphaned nails that once upon a time had supported something long since forgotten. This kitchen on a Mexican Apache ranch in the Sierra Madre, twenty-six degrees north of the equator, is a twin of a Soviet dacha kitchen of my childhood. Hilda draws me into a hug.

"There must have been Russian immigrants in the area who had come after the revolution," she says. "You know how women are. They probably went over to one another's homes to gossip or borrow provisions. They must have liked the decor."

Outside it is raining again and more people have arrived in trucks. They move about the dark garden with cell-phone flashlights on. Someone is building a fire. Someone is raising a tepee. Children and dogs chase one another in wet grass. I seek out Kiriaki Orpinel, a niece of the Holguín sisters, an anthropologist who champions the human rights of traditional societies in the Sierra Madre. Kiriaki is Rarámuri on her father's side and, as she now knows, Apache on her mother's, and we had started talking on the drive up from Ciudad Chihuahua. She is beautiful and foul-mouthed and she smokes filterless Mexican cigarettes. She was born missing her left arm below the elbow. On her right she wears charms and bracelets that jingle as she walks. Now, in the garden, we swap jewelry, my copper bracelet with rams' heads from northwest Russia for her beaded necklace in the shape of a peyote flower from northern Chihuahua. Protection amulets. She talks about Native feminism and the constricting Western interpretation of what feminism means. She describes how the agency of Rarámuri women has been eroded, first by the patriarchy of the Catholic Church, later by the patriarchy of capitalism. Talking about injustice makes her curse more and speak faster, and because my Spanish is not strong enough I often lose the thread—which is a shame, because I want to hang on to every word she says.

"Eh, doesn't matter," she says. "English, Spanish. Languages of the fucking colonizers."

I huddle with Kiriaki and her aunts under a tree, a bit out of the rain. Digging up the soil from Geronimo's grave at Fort Sill did not feel like a trespass, but here on the ranch I feel its weight, and I know it is time for Kiriaki and her aunts to have it. We stand in a circle and I palm the plastic bag over to Bernarda with both hands.

"Thank you for inviting me to your ceremony," I say, in shaky Spanish. "I brought this from the grave of Geronimo in

Oklahoma. He is buried at a cemetery for prisoners of war on an army base there. This is some soil from that place. I want you to have it."

Our circle falls inward. Like flower petals closing. For a few seconds we stand in a group embrace under the dripping tree, temple to temple in the flickering light of cell phones and bonfire. Then Kiriaki asks her aunt if she may hold the bag. She places it on the stump of her left arm and cradles it there like a baby, caresses it through the plastic.

"I didn't know he was buried in a military cemetery," she says. "Motherfuckers."

I apologize for the ziplock bag. "It's the modern way," I say. She laughs. "Postmodern," she says.

Guachochi

For the opening speeches the next day we gather on a grassy island on Lago las Garzas, a small lake in the center of town where Guachochi's health-conscious citizens walk laps at dawn. The real athletes are in the sierra: The Rarámuri, whose name means "people who run on foot," are the world's most celebrated, and possibly most exoticized, endurance runners. They routinely beat ultramarathoners from everywhere else. Four months before the ceremony, a twenty-two-year-old woman from Guachochi named María Lorena Ramírez, racing in a traditional long tiered skirt and huaraches made of tire rubber and leather strips, became the world's fastest long-distance female ultrarunner, beating five hundred other women from twelve countries in the females' fifty-kilometer category of the Ultra Trail Cerro Rojo.

The Rarámuri have been running in these mountains since the sixteenth century, when the Spanish chased them from the desert into small, remote subsistent farming communities linked by a network of narrow footpaths that drop vertiginously into canyons and climb as vertiginously. Running relays that last a day or longer are a ceremonial practice, a ritual celebration of events such as the harvest; running shorter distances, on the other hand, is a form of transportation, a quick way of getting from one place to the next. "When you run on the earth and with the earth, you can run forever," goes a Rarámuri proverb. Rarámuri runners became a mythologized global sensation after a book written by a white US journalist, *Born to Run: A Hidden Tribe, Superathletes, and the Greatest Race the World Has Never Seen*, became an international bestseller. Around the same time, cartels began hiring Rarámuri to run drugs across the border.

Two dozen Rarámuri families come to Lago las Garzas to celebrate the commencement of the ceremony. In front of a tasseled ensign embroidered with the words APACHES DESCENDIENTES DE GERÓNIMO (Geronimo's Apache Descendants) everybody exchanges greetings: the animated Holguín clan; the suited officials from the Guachochi tourism department, which is sponsoring the event; the guests from abroad: a Lipan Apache activist and filmmaker from Austin; a Tewa Hopi medicine man from Arizona; a Scandinavian documentary filmmaker duo; a husband-and-wife team of Lipan Apache lecturers from Lubbock, Texas, who travel around North America with two tepees in their truck; Roberto and Jessica and I. Three men in cowboy hats and boots and large buckles stand leaning against a park bench in that fashion men in cowboy hats and boots and large buckles like to lean against things. Every new arrival shakes hands with everyone already here, as is the custom; young girls in ribbon skirts and skinny jeans proffer their cheeks to be kissed. A woman asks me if she can take my photo with her phone. After the rounds of greetings the Rarámuri retreat to clusters, keep to themselves. Is it the linguistic divide, I ask Kiriaki.

"Linguistic, no," she says. "Racial, yes." She rubs her forefinger against her bare forearm. "It's the skin tone. Like everywhere in the world."

After two hours of speeches by the lake—the abundance of introductory speeches once more takes me back to my Soviet childhood—the Holguíns and all of us out-of-town guests climb into minivans and trucks and caravan past eleven miles of apple orchards and cornfields to the Sinforosa Canyon. From the overlook at the rim, the green vertebrae of the Sierra Madre crash down in grandiose near-vertical crags. Down down down, as deep as the Grand Canyon, past the caves where the Geronimo-Holguíns once lived, past Rarámuri running paths, past goat pastures, past marijuana plantations, down to the invisible Río Verde and her avocado groves—then up again, cresting in every direction. Tattered clouds cling to distant mesas. Cenozoic lava droolings dribble down the sides of 250-million-year-old rock that buckled and folded and faulted to become what the locals call the Queen of All Canyons. Eras collapse here. Five centuries of European conquest are no more than a fleck. A red-tailed hawk hangs on an air thermal just below the rim.

"I remember visiting these caves," says Hilda Holguín. "We still had relatives living there in the sixties. They didn't feel like moving out. They were that poor."

Or maybe they were still that afraid.

We are hungry. We load into vans and trucks again and drive back to town, where the tourism department has hired a Rarámuri folk-dance troupe to perform for us and a caterer to prepare us a fish fry. The dance and the fish fry—a rare trout that, we are told, can only be found in these mountains—will take place by the waterfall.

The Sinforosa Canyon took my breath away. But I am not prepared for the waterfall. My heart's eye is not prepared. I don't have the vocabulary for it, this sixty-two-foot wall of atomized astonishment. Bernarda shuttles between her guests, hugs us one after another, watches our reaction. "Do you like it?" she asks. "Do you like it?"

After the waterfall, Gina, Hilda, Roberto, Jessica, and I pile into a van once more. Clouds ball up in crevasses below Guachochi. We the norteños are tired, but our driver, Bernarda's youngest son, Ángel, a professional tour operator, insists on showing us around town. From the back of the van Gina and Hilda narrate the landmarks:

"This is the first church of Guachochi."

"This is the neighborhood where they say witches lived in the olden days."

"This is where, when they were laying sewage pipe, people found mammoth tusks."

"This is the airfield. It was founded by three of our brothers."

"They were the first pilots in Guachochi."

"All three died in airplane crashes."

Of course they were. Of course they did. We are in rarified air above the clouds, with Geronimo's descendants whose foremothers hid in caves and who go blind looking for truth. This is Gabriel García Márquez territory. Every eccentricity, every facet of beauty and tragedy is magnified here.

The airfield is empty; the town's only biplane is elsewhere. Can we go now? No, Ángel says, we must see the tiger. Come on, let's go.

What tiger? What kind of a joke is this? Ángel ushers us out of the van and into the terminal building that feels like someone's home, through a kitchen where a man (an off-duty pilot? an airport guard? Ángel makes no introductions) is heating up quesadillas on a stovetop, and into a patio. There is a wire-mesh fence. On the other side of the fence, under an awning behind a bed of ginger flowers and a kiddie pool that serves as her watering hole, lies a Bengal tiger.

"She belongs to my friend, who owns the plane," Ángel says. "Go ahead, you can take pictures."

Later, an artist whose work focuses on how we commodify nature explains to me man's ancient desire to own alpha predators: "What does it say about the power of possession; what status is created or projected through the 'things' we own?" To cage a tiger for amusement and display, she says, is to demonstrate domination. Just as it is to cage a resistance hero and display him at an inaugural parade, for a good show. In real-life Macondo, metaphors are as blunt as a fist in the face.

The Forest

The Crown Dancers are five in number. They are big men, with much flesh. They wear black masks and tall headdresses made of wood slats and they run out of the forest naked except for buckskin loincloths adorned with bells. They ululate and growl and one of them is whirling a bull-roarer. They gyrate and stomp and run at us and away. They are a terrifying link between the natural and the supernatural worlds, and they lunge and stomp violently and ferociously to the accelerating drumbeat to summon mountain spirits that heal and protect. They bring awe and hope. On the overcast morning of the second day of the Ceremonia del Perdón, the day after the lakeside speeches and the waterfall and the airport tiger, they bring rain and lightning and thunder upon the forest clearing where we have gathered under ponderosa pines charred by electric storms past, and young madrones forever shedding some hurt, and massive rocks patinated with lichen, and at some imperceptible signal women one by one begin to orbit their centrifugal tempest, and suddenly most women, men, children, in jeans and ponchos and traditional dress and rain slickers, in moccasins and rain boots and sandals and smart city shoes, wet and tripping over low brush, are dancing, dancing, dancing in a wide sidestepping clockwise circle.

The Crown Dancers and their drummers came from the White Mountain Apache Tribe's reservation in Arizona. Their journey took four days instead of two; their truck broke down in the mud at least twice. It is a small miracle, they tell us, that they didn't get washed down some arroyo along the way to the waterlogged heart of Mexico. Then again, it is a miracle they could dance at all. In the early 1900s the United States outlawed ceremonial Indian dances. The Crown Dance, an important Apache healing ritual, was banned and had to be taught and practiced in secrecy for generations, until the American Indian Religious Freedom Act of 1978.

The resurgent push for Indigenous rights and sovereignty has unified around the revitalization of such rituals and ceremonies as much as around the issues of environmental integrity and representation and clean water and sacred sites. "Some say that ever since these ceremonial practices were outlawed they have never been quite the same," writes the blogger Noah Nez, whose website, Native Skeptic, examines Native American spirituality. Perhaps some authenticity was lost in police-state isolation; I am not the one to judge. To me, an outsider, the Ceremonia del Perdón feels, as Kiriaki said, postmodern.

There are Rarámuri priests with shakers and a sacred malted drink in an earthenware jug. There is a tepee from Texas next to a Mexican flag. There is an amped mic, and two considerate portajohns, and speakers quoting the Colombian journalist Claudia Palacios (Bernarda: "To forgive is not to forget") and the Chilean filmmaker Alejandro Jodorowsky (Kiriaki: "The past is not fixed and unalterable. With faith and will we can change it, not erasing its darkness but adding lights to it to make it more and more beautiful, the way a diamond is cut").

There are the Crown Dancers, spirits incarnate and awesome; and there are the lay dancers: Bernarda and Hilda and Gina and Kiriaki. Roberto and Ángel and his sister Hillary, who is sixteen. The Tewa Hopi medicine man, and the Lipan Apache lecturers with the tepees, and Fox RedSky, an activist from Austin, a US Army veteran and a veteran of both the monthslong standoff at Standing Rock and the Keystone XL pipeline protest, who is making a documentary about the Native tribes of Texas, of which only three are federally recognized.

Fox likes a hip-hop song called "All Nations Rise," by the Diné singer Lyla June. Toward the end of the song June declaims: "They say that history is written by the victors / But how can there be a victor when the war isn't over?" Think of post-conquest American history as an ongoing five-hundred-year-long insurgency against invaders who stamp out this uprising over and over with varying degrees of brutality and self-congratulatory blindness. When Geronimo was a teenager, US forces rounded up nearly all the Native people east of the Mississippi, seventy thousand in all, and marched them to Indian Territory along what is now known as the Trail of Tears. At least one out of five perished during that ethnic cleansing campaign. Within the next two decades, two-thirds of the Native population of gold-rush California died of enslavement, starvation, reservation confinement, and targeted killing. Then came the genocidal massacres of the Indian Wars.

In this history, who is Geronimo? Colonial mythology exoticizes him either as the last great Native American freedom fighter or as the most violent holdout of the Indian Wars; the US military picked the code name "Geronimo" for the operation to capture Osama bin Laden. But do you see a twenty-eight-year-old suddenly widowed, orphaned, and childless all at once? Do you see a father in a country where the government pays bounties for scalps of children?

The Holguíns are lighting a ceremonial flame in a pedestal grill, to prevent a forest fire. One of Geronimo's many possible great-great-grandsons, Alex Holguín, hands out pieces of paper and pencils. Bernarda has explained her idea for this: "It is a ceremony to ask God to forgive, in the name of our ancestors, the perpetrators and the victims. We will ask for forgiveness for the wars against Indians. For the turbulent times the consequences of which we are still suffering today." People are lining up to torch their pain. In the rain, smoke over the grill billows white.

I guess forgiveness means making peace. But on this day, in the forest, I don't think it is my place to make peace. Then Hilda Holguín approaches with a disposable plate loaded with what she calls "Apache food"—a stew of potatoes, onions, hot dogs, and ground meat cooked up in an enormous communal vat—and says, "All these things I have, they form me. I, too, didn't have anything I wanted to forgive or reclaim in the fire. But my sisters really wanted me to write something and burn it. So I did. For my sisters. Because it is important to them, and they are important to me."

A man comes by to watch over my shoulder as I take notes. I have seen him at other events, in Guachochi.

"Very good," he says. "All very clear what you write."

"Thank you."

"Are you writing everyone here?"

"Excuse me?"

"Are you writing everyone at this forgiveness?"

"Trying to, yes."

"Then you have to write me too. Write down my name too. José Luís González. From Guachochi. Write it."

And I do.

I do not know what happened to the soil I brought from Fort Sill in a ziplock bag. I do not ask. In Guachochi, among the

Holguíns, the soil from Geronimo's grave is not a historical event. It is a private matter.

Guachochi to Ciudad Chihuahua

I leave Guachochi the following dawn. I take a bus. It is a long day down the mountains; for the first three hours we weave above clouds. I take an aisle seat in the back. For a while a young woman sits in the window seat next to mine. She is wearing bright pink slacks, a purple faux-leather bomber jacket, and dark blue earbuds connected to a pink Nokia phone, one of the earlier smartphone models that still has push buttons; she keeps it on top of a leatherette purse with a busy floral design. From time to time she dips into the purse for corn chips, rustles their loud Mylar bag. An hour or so outside Guachochi she squeezes past me with a smile and walks toward the bus door in the front. A few minutes later the bus stops to let her out on a curve. I take her seat; now I can look out the window. Slowly we pull forward and a minute or so later I see her in the piñon forest. She is sprinting down a path faster than any athlete I have ever seen, left hand holding her purse to her body, right hand slicing the air, a pink-and-purple spirit, a modern woman running about her life.

Dark Matter

THERE ARE NO CATTLE on the ranch, though my landlady does have several cats. Beyond the wire fence is wilderness, high desert; wilderness inside the ranch, too. There are mule deer and white-tailed deer with translucent ears at dawn, a fox in the carport, a woodpecker metronoming the mesquite tree all day, mourning doves, owls by night. One morning, I leave open the door of my rental casita and a javelina walks in, walks out. Another morning, a blue grosbeak hurtles into the window glass, streaks to the ground, an indigo comet. I am on the other side of the window, at my desk; I run out, palm him, shush steady his heartbeat against my life line. The book I am writing is set on the Atlantic coast of Africa, and I tell the grosbeak about the sea on my page, the sea as blue as his mantle. In the desert it is quite normal to speak to birds.

Outside the ranch fence, sometimes pronghorn pass in the light. Pronghorn are the world's fastest mammals over long distances, they can sustain a speed of sixty miles per hour for hours on end; their eyes can see three hundred degrees; they can detect movement four miles away. Pronghorn, *Antilocapra americana*, are the only surviving species of the Antilocapridae family—and barely. Estimated in the range of thirty-five million head in the early 1800s, pronghorn were largely hunted out to feed European settlers and construction crews that made possible the westward takeover of the continent. Their habitats were ransacked, their migration routes disarranged, truncated, cut off. By the late twentieth century only twelve thousand head remained: those that outran the extinction, or outsaw it. I believe them to be a miracle.

Pronghorn will not jump a fence. Fences are recent, not yet a part of their ancient language of survival. Pronghorn are fenced out of the ranch, but that means they are fenced in on the ranch that abuts it, because fences tesserate this desert, unseam it with barbed wire and concertina wire and cattle guards and rail fences and deer-fence mesh and steel-rod walls around ranches and fracking sites and pipeline trenches, around concentration camps for migrants, along the border eighty miles to the south. Each year, more fences. Roberto Lujan, the retired teacher who grew up down the road from the ranch, tells me how, in the 1960s, vaqueros would walk through town hollering, ¡*Que viva la sierra*!—and others would shout back, ¡*Y que no me la encierren*! When he tells me this, his voice quivers.

Anglo settlers took up residence here in the 1880s, and that's when official historical records say the town was established, but people have lived here for at least ten thousand years. An archaeologist shows a group of us a place on someone else's ranch that he says is one of the oldest episodically inhabited sites in the area. He explains how to date a tepee circle, an ancient fire pit, an arrowhead. The first people hunted; then they ranched; then came a train; then a small university named after a Confederate general. Now there is also a movie theater and a laundromat with an adjacent coffee shop; the coffee shop is overpriced but where else would you wait out the spin cycle, in the desert? Fewer than six thousand people live here, and everyone waves hello, but there is man in town who, when I wave, coos back: *Hoo! Hoo!* A lonesome sound, high-pitched, like a mourning dove. Sometimes he sees me first and comes close and—*Hoo! Hoo!*—startles me with his bird lament. Sometimes I laugh. One morning he pops up in the dairy aisle of the little grocer. *Hoo! Hoo!* Before I can wave at him or say anything back he has vanished in the direction of the cleaning products. I think he is being playful, but who knows? "If only the birds had subtitles," writes Alice Oswald.

Down the road from the ranch, a neighbor has spray-painted on the wall of one shed the words IN CASE OF ZOMBIES and on another JESUS IS LORD. The Jesus line is written in loose, white block letters; the one about zombies is stenciled neatly onto pale zinc. Read consecutively, the way I do when I ride past on my bicycle, the words seem to offer a warning (zombies may happen) and a solution (turn to Jesus, somehow). Or they may be a kind of an implicatured declaration of faith: Never mind the zombies, we'll be saved. Or, possibly, there is no connection between the messages, only a spatial continuity; that would make the Jesus part a garden-variety tagline, the zombie part a joke.

The inscriptions become idée fixe after a community organization asks me to write about words I "see everyday" for a summer literary initiative. "By encouraging people to pay closer attention to their surroundings," reads the emailed explanation, this initiative "invites an exchange of stories about who we are and where we come from." I like the assignment: The project seems to enjoin communality in a world where so many of us come from elsewhere, like me, and where so much fences us apart. Besides, I like puzzling out the meanings of things, imagining what else is there. Maybe the words are instructions to what the sheds contain? I imagine the inside of the Jesus shed, cobbled out of patches of corrugated rust and painted haint blue: crucifixes, candle-wax stalagmites, bottles of communion wine, maybe an entire small chapel. And in the other, a newish zinc prefab, anti-zombie weapons—let's see, what would those be? I google it: assault rifles, the kind people use to kill one another in wars, the kind that, the month after I first move to town, Omar Mateen uses to murder forty-nine people at a gay nightclub in Orlando, Florida.

Thanks to conservation efforts, the pronghorn population in the United States now exceeds one million, and the Texas herds are densest on the Marfa Plateau, where I am renting my casita. Now you can hunt pronghorn again, and several companies in the area will assist you. One has an online brochure that features photographs of people sitting and kneeling next to dead pronghorn bucks. In most photographs, the people are holding up the animals' heads by the horns in such a way that the pronghorn look alive, as if they just decided to lie down there for a minute, to pose next to these humans, why not, look, the humans are smiling. In the background—high desert, a mesquite tree. For $4,300, the brochure says, the outfit will provide you with lodging, three freshly cooked meals a day, and guides who will help you track the pronghorn and then skin, cape, and quarter the carcass. The brochure warns that you might leave empty-handed. "No guarantees." "Due to the nature of hunting." This preserves an element of the ineffable. Texas law prohibits hunting with fully automatic weapons, but you can hunt pronghorn with an assault rifle as long as you use a suppressor.

There is a smaller herd north of here, toward El Paso; I often see it by the highway when I drive that way. When Patrick Crusius takes that highway to shoot dead twenty-three people at an El Paso Walmart with a Romanian-built Kalashnikov assault rifle, is the herd there, does he notice it?

Among the things I have learned about violence is that it requires no imagination or evolutionary advancement: It is basically effective. This makes all the more strange our perpetual surprise in the face both of the violence and of our inherent predisposition toward it. It is as if we are under-evolved somehow, as if violence is a fence that has only just been erected in our path, not a condition we have sustained since prehistory. As if we are living in a foreign language: Individual words make sense, but we still strain to coalesce meaning.

Four billion years ago, a multimillion-year rain rained an ocean to flood the whole of Hadean earth. After the ocean receded, for almost a hundred million years the Marfa Plateau remained submerged. The desert here is the exposed bottom of a vanished sea, the Delaware. Mountains cardiogram it: dusky purple, robin's-egg blue, gunmetal black. To the west of the ranch, a collapsed caldera puckers its ancient keloid at the long sky.

To the northeast blues a buildup of reef and limestone from two hundred and sixty million years ago. Farther out, Paleozoic rocks slump toward a chaparral plateau. This desert was drowned, kneaded, jabbed, blistered, ruptured, choked with ash for half a billion years of geologic tumult. You can almost see the latent power of these violent tectonics.

Today water here comes from a minor aquifer trapped in a volcanic rock hollow: a thirty-five-million-year-old stilled lava capsule. The aquifer recharges, but very slowly: Rain is rare here and getting rarer, and what does not evaporate right off takes its time to seep through all the layers of dirt and volcanic ash and limestone and granite and rhyolite and basalt. This bolson is the sole source of water for three sizable towns set on a nearly equilateral triangle about twenty-five miles apart. I cook and bathe with water from this underground freshwater sea, which my landlady's windmill pump lifts from a well two hundred and fifty feet deep. On windy days the ungreased pump on the ranch bellows rusty ballads. My landlady has christened it the Elephant. I can see the Elephant from the kitchen window of the casita when I prepare meals.

What color was the sea after the Hadean cloud cover thinned, lifted, and the sun shone upon the newborn skin of water for the very first time? Blue as the grosbeak, as the sea in Senegal, or Homeric, wine-dark? And what color is the invisible freshwater sea beneath me, the one I drink from and cook and wash with, in that igneous bubble of the aquifer?

The aquifer's depth varies through the region. Some people have to drill six hundred feet underground before they hit the bolson.

My landlady and my neighbors worry about water. Oil and gas companies are poking the desert for fossil fuel, bore it with pipelines to transport what they dig up. Some of what they dig up is what I cook with, on a three-burner gas stove pilfered from a 1950s trailer. The gas line for the stove runs through a hole in the kitchen wall to a propane can that stands on an antique wooden chair outside the kitchen window. I tell myself that this setup is perfectly safe, just as the oil and gas companies tell us their pipelines are perfectly safe.

Those of us who join the archaeologist at the prehistoric site are the last people ever to see the ten-thousand-year-old ashpits and tepee circles. The next morning mulchers and bulldozers trench the ancestral grounds to make way for a gas pipeline.

Full moon in May. Night. Screeching like bloodshed. Under my writing window. Behind the casita. On the other side of the casita. Then comes a thump on the front door—or maybe I dream it and wake up.

In the morning, putting on my running shoes, I hear from above a kind of rasping. What kind of bird would that be? I step outside and look up into the ash tree that grows to the north side of the door. Two raccoons, tetchy post-coitus, glare down at me.

Over drinks at sunset my landlady tells me one of her cats is having an affair with the fox.

Twenty-five miles northwest of the ranch, at the northern tip of the bolson, sits the Hobby-Eberly Telescope, one of the world's largest, with an aperture of thirty feet, designed specifically to decode light from stars and galaxies billions of light-years ago. Scientists who work on it study dark energy, the phenomenon of the accelerating universe—which is to say, why we are here and where we are going. They stare ten billion years back in space. From such an old sky they strain to gauge the meaning and mystery of life.

The Hobby-Eberly Telescope's mirror is always tilted at the same angle, fifty-five degrees above the horizon. Flaring from the new oil wells a few miles away extends directly into its target field, interferes with the darkness and the telescope's existential inquiry. Scientists have observed a fifty percent increase in light pollution since the drilling began. Our astronomical yearning and our astronomical desire for wealth collide in the desert.

A young woman technician repairs and replaces the composite mirrors on the big telescope. Her name is Katie. She must physically crawl into the iron lattice that supports the mirrors to exchange the ones that became smeared with bird feathers, bug splats, and bat guano overnight, when the telescope roof was open.

If Katie doesn't clean the mirrors, scientists may not know dark matter from bat shit.

For the most part, surface water in the desert comes as condensation. On summer mornings I watch the desert sun burn dew off nopal spines. There were nopal thickets in Senegal, too, trafficked there on ships sailing triangle trade winds, cargoed collaterally, like haint blue, or zombies. The general after whom the town university was named, one of the youngest in the Confederacy, fought one hundred and thirty-five battles and skirmishes in the name of such debasement. Look how violence connects us, fences us in, prisms in angled morning light.

The world speaks to us in symbols: bluebirds, nopal plants, pronghorn, zombies. There are no bad symbols just as there are no bad words, there are merely the billion hurts we inflict upon one another, the billion comforts we bestow. I begin to think that the words on my neighbor's shed are a kind of prayer, an elegy for the world we are so carelessly debasing, a thanksgiving for the world that still confers wonder.

I stand by the stove, I listen to the Elephant, I scan the desert for movement. There, that shadow just beyond the ranch fence—pronghorn.

In West Texas people often call pronghorn antelope. Antelope play an important role in stories about who we are and where we come from. Antelope introduced agriculture among the Bambara; they protect the Kwele from evil spirits; in the Far East, the horn of the saiga cures a variety of ailments, including impotence, the common cold, and lung disease. In the Middle East and Europe, antelope in their many iterations are symbols of resistance, elegance, and grace.

> Your breasts are two fawns,
> twins of a gazelle,
> grazing in a field of lilies,

goes the Song of Songs.

But pronghorn are not antelope; they are the only species of the Antilocapridae family, itself the only North American member of the Giraffoidea superfamily, of which indeed only three species still exist: pronghorn, okapi, and giraffe. In Senegal, as in most of West Africa, giraffe have been extirpated by early-twentieth-century hunting and mid-twentieth-century drought, but before then, French colonial authorities hired local gunmen to kill giraffe because the animals' long necks ripped down telegraph wires.

Why do we keep wanting to call something by another's name? Why refuse to address head-on the two experiences that pinnacle our humanness, violence and astonishment, why find circuitous ways to describe them; why not behold and marvel at what is before us on its own terms, just as it is; what avarice within us makes us plow right through the miraculous, or past it, without pause, makes us insatiable? Even the Song of Songs does it, with all its arabesques—but listen to how it pierces when it does not:

I am my lover's,
he longs for me,
only for me.

Pronghorn are the only animal in the world with horns that branch, shaped like an upturned cowboy boot with an extra-tapered heel, and the only horned animal that sheds horns every year. Because of their forked nature, the horns can be a good or a bad omen. A pronghorn carcass on the doorstep will grant a questing hero the support of a helper. A Diné pronghorn kachina will make the rains come and the grass grow. In a Blackfoot tradition, when Old Man created the world, he first placed pronghorn in the mountains, but the pronghorn stumbled and fell down on the rocks, so Old Man moved pronghorn to the prairie country, where it could run far and fast; that was before the fences. An Apache story says that a beautiful young woman once became a pronghorn, and her descendants still roam the earth, so if you eat a pronghorn you may be eating a relative.

The last night of December brings lightning and thunder and rain to the desert, the sky disgorging the remnants of the year. Some of this rain will help refill the bolson, sod the ranch road, rinse the fences, flood the street with the sheds so it becomes impassible by bicycle. Think of the world as tunneled and pierced by water yet at once held together by it. Think of the sea as ever-present even in the driest times and places: through the salinity of our own bodies, our blood, tears, sperm. Think of ecotones not only horizontally but vertically as well: the ecotone of cloud, the ecotone of rain. Where it hits the ground, the puzzle.

On the ranch, before bedtime, as rain pelts the rooftop, I check the news. Across the ocean, in Istanbul, an hour after midnight, a man dressed as Santa Claus walks into a nightclub. He is carrying an assault rifle. He kills thirty-nine people.

By the first dawn of the new year, all the stars shine in the squeegeed sky over the ranch and the morning is pale blue and golden, and pronghorn run in wet wilted grass.

Dark matter is what scientists believe holds galaxies together, keeps them from ripping out of our universe, grants the universe the gravity to stay intact. Dark matter is invisible; it does not interact with electromagnetic force; scientists have not yet been able to detect it. It is, put simply, beyond our ken, the way the meaning and value of life and the loss of it are ultimately beyond our ken; or the cosmic consequence of despoiling civilizations, living or premodern; or animals extirpated by our recklessness; or animals that miraculously survive it. What is the universal gravity of what we cannot see, or of what we cannot ever see again? Look, the evening desert exhales wetly into the indigo dark—and in the distance, a hint of starward motion, something ascending.

Jericho

I HEAR MY FIRST TULSA TRUMPET the day I move to the city. It is a Saturday in January. The man sits on a bench on the corner across the street from my apartment, presses his lips against the mouthpiece in such bitter cold. Like maybe he can keep warm by touching his mouth to brass the color of fire. He is playing Nat Adderley's "Work Song" on repeat.

> Hold it steady right there while I hit it
> Well, reckon that ought to get it

Around us, the red brick right angles of a century-old lynching site are being gentrified into a tightly curated hipster haven. Where a pogromed neighborhood once burned there are now luxury apartment blocks and galleries and yoga studios and a baseball field; a bakery called Antoinette's displays a window sign that reads EAT CAKE. The neighborhood, like much of Tulsa, again smells like something burning, from the oil refineries that rim the city. I cannot tell if by choosing "Work Song" the man on the corner is flipping a bird at all this cognitive dissonance or playing along with it or both.

The oldest trumpets known to man were found in the pharaoh Tutankhamun's tomb in 1922. They are more than thirty-three hundred years old. They are about twenty inches long, straight like Greek salpinges; the Pied Piper of Hamelin is believed to have played an instrument shaped the same way. In 1939 the BBC recorded the bandsman James Tappern of the 11th Royal Hussars playing them. Tappern used his own mouthpiece to perform something like a fanfare based on the "Posthorn Gallop" by Hermann Koenig, the twentieth-century brass-band darling. But the music on the recording is not the "Posthorn Gallop." No. There is something queasy about the sound. It wobbles, bends anxiously. It throbs. It is terrifying, terrible. It floods my gut like a malarial dream. The Pied Piper's horn must have sounded like this.

A trumpet: originally a signaling device: a shofar, an abeng. "Instruments used in war to frighten the enemy," the ninth-century philosopher and musical theorist Abu Nasr Muhammad ibn Muhammad al Farabi wrote in his *Grand Book of Music*, "are very loud and unbearable to the human ear."

There is a legend that the pharaoh's trumpets are cursed with the power to unloose war. People who believe this legend point out that each of the three times the trumpets were blown since being exhumed, catastrophe followed: first World War II, then the first Gulf War, then the Egyptian Revolution of 2011. This may be apophenia. In the history of human violence there is always a war somewhere to match the blow of a horn.

Ever do we breathe meaning into sound, sound into things. For about a decade, scholars believed the oldest known existing instrument to be the Divje Babe flute, a piece of bear femur about five inches long that may be as old as sixty-seven thousand years, which would have made it the only found musical instrument of the Neanderthals—except then tests determined that the Divje Babe flute, discovered in a Slovenian cave, was merely a bone chewed up, likely by a hyena, not a musical instrument. Now the consensus is that the earliest found musical instruments are the flutes some *Homo sapiens*, in what today is Germany, whittled between forty-two and forty-three thousand years ago of mammoth ivory and swan bone.

I saw a swan-bone flute in Tbilisi, Georgia, in a museum. It dates back to the twelfth or eleventh century BCE, about as old as the Trojan War, or the Olmec civilization, or Nebuchadnezzar. It is almost eight inches long. It is silvery gray, slightly bowed, polished to a sheen, unreeded, and has only three holes, and it was found alongside the body of a boy who died at the age of fourteen or fifteen. The Soviet academician who found the burial site in 1938 called the place the Grave of the Little Shepherd. What was it like, the devastation of that swan-bone flute in the velvet dark of the Georgian Caucasus three thousand years ago, that Little Shepherd's swan song?

Once, in northern Afghanistan, I heard a little shepherd's flute in the ruins of the city Alexander the Great had built for his Afghan trophy wife, Roxanne, in 328 BCE, a thousand years after Tutankhamun, eight or nine hundred years after the Georgian boy. Little remains of Alexandria Oxiana: In the course of two millennia, invaders from all over have sacked the palace, bombed the bathhouse, used the limestone curlicues of Corinthian columns for target practice. There is a hint of a perfectly round theater where wild garlic sprouts through shards of pottery and sheep droppings in a circular field, and fragments of columns glow white among overgrown rectangles of mid-twentieth-century excavations that were abandoned because of war, first one, then another; occasionally people find intact things here, a figurine, a small vessel, a piece of jewelry. And the name Afghans call the place: Ai Khanum, Lady Moon. I have visited it several times since I first stayed on a nearby farm in the autumn of 2001, in the beginning of the latest invasion of the Khorasan by the United States. My most recent visit was almost a decade later, in early spring. The

war was still going on. I was in the area to see my former landlord, a farmer who used to smuggle antique artifacts he found
at Ai Khanum and fence them to visiting merchants until the
post-Taliban government clamped down on the trade. We
drove to Ai Khanum together.

A steady drizzle fell on the ruins when we arrived. The plateau was flat, cold. Sparrows banked on gusts of wind. That
was when I heard the flute. A dirge, a skein of child grief, so
singular my heart broke.

We passed the little shepherd on our drive back to my former
landlord's farm. He and two other boys were sitting on a spring-
green hilltop, in the wet grass, watching some cattle and sheep.
The one with the flute was the oldest and looked about eight,
but I know that age is elusive when it comes to sound: He had
been sitting there since before Alexander and his Lady Moon,
he is still sitting there, he will sit there forever.

Even if a hyena's teeth and not a man's tool bore the perfectly
round openings in the Divje Babe flute, how can we know for
sure that some Neanderthal didn't play the thing? That it did
not make music? That it didn't undo all those who heard it?

I don't know why the Little Shepherd of Georgia died before reaching adulthood. Tutankhamun, who also died a teenager, likely died of malaria. Almost half a million people still die of malaria each year, mostly children. One child every thirty seconds: Say it out loud, is it bearable to your ear?

Al Farabi, who wrote the *Grand Book of Music* and also treatises on metaphysics, ethics, and logic, and whom Avicenna considered his teacher, lived in Baghdad, Damascus, and Egypt. He died either in Aleppo or in Damascus, in the middle of the tenth century. Where was he from? No one knows anymore. Al Farabi means "from Farab," but the location of the Farab of his birth is disputed: Farab is a common Persian name for a town built near a system of irrigation canals and qanats. In the Middle Ages at least three Central Asian localities were called Farab. One was in what today is Kazakhstan; another in modern-day Turkmenistan, downstream on the River Oxus from Ai Khanum. Or, al Farabi could have hailed from Faryab in Afghanistan; if so, then the chicory-flecked hills of his birthplace had heard the war trumpets of Alexander's eastbound army as it rolled toward Ai Khanum, including a legendary monster trumpet that is said to have measured five cubits, or nearly eight feet, in diameter, had to be managed by sixty men, and could be heard at the distance of a hundred stadia, which is more than eleven miles.

I have been ill with malaria several times, including once in Faryab. I had just sat down to interview a minor warlord in the parlor of his house, where he received me surrounded by a platoon of his men, when I felt suddenly and violently ill. I shot out of the room but not fast enough and ended up being sick all over the small army of boots and sandals that belonged to the warlord and his soldiers, who had brought their assault rifles and rocket-propelled grenade launchers into the parlor with them, but had left their footwear just outside the front door as tradition dictates. I remember the surge of shame before I blacked out on top of my mess. I have little recollection of the days and nights of delirium that followed, other than that the warlord, whose name I had written down in a notebook I have since lost, had graciously allowed me to convalesce in his house despite my having soiled everyone's shoes, and that after someone had rigged an IV drip from a ceiling beam I hallucinated a paisley world of sonorous light plumes.

Humans blew trumpets in ancient Africa, Central Asia, Greece, Rome, and the Levant. (My God, the distress of their queer call across that swath of the earth!) About a hundred and fifty years before Tutankhamun was buried with his trumpets, Israelites blew trumpets outside the walls of Jericho—though their trumpets most likely were shofars, ram horns like the one that had made them tremble in awe before God revealed the Ten Commandments to Moses at Mount Sinai.

Go blow them ram horns Joshua cried
'Cause the devil can't do you no harm.

Until the fourteenth century of our era, trumpets were one- or two-toned instruments "not known to have been used in music," according to *The New Harvard Dictionary of Music.* "They remained instruments . . . for signaling, announcing, commanding, and ceremonial purposes."

But what is music if not a command? The second time I hear a trumpet in Tulsa I am crossing the railroad tracks on the Boston Avenue Pedestrian Bridge. Dark evening in late winter, cold prairie wind dense with petrochemicals and sorrow—and then the doors of the old depot open and there it is. A brass summons; I enter. Inside, a mostly older crowd, standing or sitting around some tables, nodding as a jazz band plays, ambitiously, "Blue in Green." One couple dancing—sailing is the word really, their moves understated, minimal, not so much moves as signifiers of moves, the way a dance can become for two people who have been dancing together for half a century. I find a place to stand in the back, behind one of the old repurposed wooden train-station benches; in front of me a man senses my presence, turns his head, we nod, here we are together, the music's good, good to be here, out of the cold and the stink, here on the bridge above the wounded suppurating city.

No walls come tumbling down at the jazz depot; outside, Tulsa castles recalcitrant. But the Tuesday night jam at the Oklahoma Jazz Hall of Fame becomes my weekly comfort, my space-time of querencia, a place to make and meet friends, an oasis that sits above the railway that splits the city, segregates the wronged side of the tracks.

been
working and working
but I still got so terribly far to go

One of my favorite horn players is the jazz composer Ibrahim Maalouf. Born in Beirut, he fled civil war as a child and grew up in France. His trumpet has a fourth valve, for quarter tones, but it is not the extra valve that makes his sound unmistakable: It is that when he plays he loosens his embouchure to let just a little bit of air escape between his lips and the mouthpiece, making the sound start so airy it is almost sloppy—but once he hits a note he stiffens the lips again and tongues the mouthpiece like he is talking to it, like he is making love, going down on it, persistent and gentle at once, that's it, mm-hmm, that's it right there, please oh please don't stop, make her sing.

The common view that jazz is acceptable and often sophisticated music is relatively recent. In February 1921, three months before a white mob lynched and burned Black Tulsa, the Princeton professor of English Henry van Dyke, a white man, told a national convention of educators in New Jersey: "Jazz music was invented by demons for the torture of imbeciles." But by then jazz had already suffused the world. Forty-three hundred miles away, in Leningrad, both my paternal grandfather and his brother, Uncle Lyonya, played in jazz bands in the 1930s—my grandfather played the trumpet, and Uncle Lyonya, the saxophone. Early Soviet leaders saw jazz as socially righteous music, a tool of political struggle of the oppressed African Americans. My grandfather soon switched to conducting a light orchestra, and Uncle Lyonya was drafted and shipped off to war—to two wars, one after the other, both in the gauzy forests of Karelia. The Soviet invasion of Finland began in late November 1939 and ended in mid-March 1940; the Finns call it Talvisota, the Winter War. Uncle Lyonya would have been discharged in 1942, and maybe would have gone back to playing jazz, except in 1941 Hitler had invaded the Soviet Union and there were no demobilizations. Uncle Lyonya remained a soldier until 1946, and then the Kremlin decided that jazz was a propaganda tool for the bourgeois decadence of the West and banned it, and outlawed the saxophone. Uncle Lyonya became an engineer, sold the saxophone, and never played again.

Trumpets did not make the walls of Jericho fall, the human voice did. "And when the army heard the trumpet sound, they raised a great shout, and down fell the walls," reads the Old Testament—or, as the spiritual has it, "Old Joshua shouted glory / And the walls came tumblin' down." The human voice was the first musical instrument, before the swan-bone flute. No musical instrument, according to al Farabi, is more perfect than the voice.

It begins on the other side of the Atlantic, on the continent where, as far as we know, everything human began, our love and our violence and our dreaming and our music. It begins as the slightest tremolo, a capillary ripple, not a song but a hint of a song, a song being born. It is being born right here before me, on a night terrace in a colonial city built mostly on water, built maybe even *of* water, a vanishing city that the rising ocean is slowly licking back into the waves even as the song unravels above the unraveling coastline like the gill net the city's fishers unfurl in the sea to comb the waves for fish.

Like Alexander's fallen metropolis, the city has two names. The Wolof call it Ndar, the name it had before the French invaded it, renamed it Saint-Louis, and turned it into the capital of French West African colonies, from which they cargoed people to the New World. Maybe the ancestors of the Tulsa trumpet player, too, had fished this coastline, maybe the grandfathers of the people whose two-toned abengs urgenced rebellion in the Blue Mountains, too, had sung on these shores.

Two men are casting their voices into the night, a baritone and a falsetto. Their set begins with a song that, in turn, begins with the Shahada, the foundational recitation of faith. Most people in Ndar are Sufi, and Sufi Muslims believe that music can help you achieve proximity to God, that the ultimate truth can be found in the obliteration of the self through high mystical ecstasy, and that mystical ecstasy may be achieved through song. Ceremonial purposes. The men hang the diaphanous net of their song in the dark where it coruscates, glitters. It is like holding your breath, like holding a bird in your hand. Over the terrace in Ndar a full moon rises, a seawall yields to the surf's embouchure, and I understand.

Notes

Versions of some of these essays first appeared in *Emergence, Granta, The New York Review of Books, Opossum, The Paris Review*, and *Warscapes*. Poetry lines by Mahealani Perez-Wendt are used by permission. The author is grateful for the support of the John. F. Simon Guggenheim Memorial Foundation during the writing of this book.

ONCE I TOOK A WEEKLONG WALK IN THE SAHARA

28 *most distracted messenger I know*: Alice Oswald, *Nobody* (London: Cape Poetry, 2019).

THE PANDEMIC, OUR COMMON STORY

41 *impoverishment and degradation*: W. G. Sebald, *The Emigrants* (New York: New Directions, 2016).

42 *which isn't what it should be*: W. G. Sebald, *The Emergence of Memory* (New York: Seven Stories Press, 2010).

47 *the wages of dying is love*: Galway Kinnell, "Little Sleep's-Head Sprouting Hair in the Moonlight," *The Book of Nightmares* (Boston: Houghton Mifflin Company, 1971).

49 *Adam's Lament carries a kind of guidance*: This version of Adam's Lament, quoted below, is from Archimandrite Sophrony, *Saint Silouan the Athonite*, translated by Rosemary Edmonds (Madlon, UK: Stavropegic Monastery of St. John the Baptist, 1991): "I have grieved my beloved God! . . . I cannot forget Him for a single moment, and my soul

languishes after Him, and from the multitude of my afflictions I lift
up my voice and cry: 'Have mercy upon me, O God. Have mercy on
Thy fallen creature.'"

HOW TO READ THE AIR

59 *they're making monster sounds*: *Antigonick (Sophokles)*, translated
by Anne Carson (New York: New Directions, 2012).

60 *even to the individual concerned*: Margaret A. Boden, "Creativity
as a Neuroscientific Mystery," in *Neuroscience of Creativity*, edited by
Oshin Vartanian, Adam S. Bristol, and James C. Kaufman (Cambridge,
MA: The MIT Press, 2013).

61 *has been hit by a tautology*: Joseph Brodsky, "The Condition We
Call Exile," in *On Grief and Reason* (New York: Farrar, Straus and Gri-
oux, 1995).

63 *down to its BAM BAM BAM*: *Agamemnon* by Aiskhylos, in *An Orestiea*,
translated by Anne Carson (New York: Farrar, Straus and Giroux,
2009).

63 *Does she have a brain*: Ibid.

65 *everywhere, up to now*: Galway Kinnell, "Wait," in *Mortal Acts,
Mortal Words* (New York: Houghton Mifflin Company, 1980).

WAYS OF SEEING

78 *skip the funerals*: Morgan Parker, "If you are over staying woke," in
Magical Negro: Poems (Brooklyn, NY: Tin House Books, 2019).

82 *Earth movers, / And shovelers*: Mahealani Perez-Wendt, "Bury Our
Hearts at Wal-Mart, etc.," in *Papahanaumoku*, Allison Hedge Coke,
editor (London: Earthworks/Salt Publishing, 2009).

82 *or to denounce horror*: José Eduardo Agualusa, *The Book of Cha-
meleons*, translated by Daniel Hahn (New York: Simon & Schuster,
2004).

83 *but they see enormous things*: Rumi, "Untitled," *Rumi: The Big Red
Book*, translated by Coleman Barks (New York: Harper One, 2010).

LANDSCAPE WITH ICARUS

Unless otherwise noted, all translations of Ovid's *Metamorphoses* are by Rolfe Humphries (Bloomington, IN: Indiana University Press, 1960).

108 *float upon the wandering breeze*: Ovid, *Metamorphoses*, translated by A. D. Melville (Oxford: Oxford University Press, 2009).

109 *to make two wings*: Robert Hayden, "O Daedalus, Fly Away Home," in *A Ballad of Remembrance* (London: Paul Breman, 1962).

FORGIVING THE UNFORGIVABLE

135 *of those betrayed at dawn*: Zbigniew Herbert, "The Envoy of Mr. Cogito," in *Selected Poems*, translated by Bogdana and John Carpenter (Oxford: Oxford University Press, 1993).

DARK MATTER

168 *grazing in a field of lilies*: The Song of Songs, translated by Chana Bloch and Ariel Bloch (Berkeley, CA: University of California Press, 1995).

169 *only for me*: Ibid.

ANNA BADKHEN was born in the Soviet Union and is now an American citizen. She is the author of six previous books of nonfiction. She has received a Guggenheim Fellowship, a Barry Lopez Visiting Writer in Ethics and Community Fellowship, and a Joel R. Seldin Award from Psychologists for Social Responsibility for writing about civilians in war zones.